Commentary on the Book of Daniel
Bible Study Notes and Comments

by David E. Pratte

Available in print at
www.gospelway.com/sales

Commentary on the Book of Daniel:
Bible Study Notes and Comments

© Copyright David E. Pratte, 2019
All rights reserved

ISBN: 9781674165042
Imprint: Independently published

Note carefully: No teaching in any of our materials is intended or should ever be construed to justify or to in any way incite or encourage personal vengeance or physical violence against any person.

Front page photo
Daniel in the Lion's Den
(artist's conception)

Then Daniel said to the king, "O king, live forever! My God sent His angel and shut the lions' mouths, so that they have not hurt me, because I was found innocent before Him; and also, O king, I have done no wrong before you." – Daniel 6:21,22 (NKJV)

Photo credit: Public domain, via Wikimedia Commons

Other Acknowledgements

Unless otherwise indicated, Scripture quotations are generally from the New King James Version (NKJV), copyright 1982, 1988 by Thomas Nelson, Inc. used by permission. All rights reserved.

Scripture quotations marked (NASB) are from *Holy Bible, New American Standard* La Habra, CA: The Lockman Foundation, 1995.

Scripture quotations marked (ESV) are from *The Holy Bible, English Standard Version*, copyright ©2001 by Crossway Bibles, a publishing ministry of Good News Publishers. Used by permission. All rights reserved.

Scripture quotations marked (MLV) are from Modern Literal Version of The New Testament, Copyright 1999 by G. Allen Walker.

Scripture quotations marked (NRSV) are from the New Revised Standard Version of the Bible, copyright 1989 by the Division of Christian Education, National Council of the Churches of Christ in the United States of America.

Scripture quotations marked (NIV) are from the New International Version of the Holy Bible, copyright 1978 by Zondervan Bible publishers, Grand Rapids, Michigan.

Scripture quotations marked (HCSB) are from the Holman Christian Standard Bible, copyright 2008 by Holman Bible publishers, Nashville, Tennessee.

Other Books by the Author

Topical Bible Studies

Why Believe in God, Jesus, and the Bible? (evidences)
True Words of God: Bible Inspiration and Preservation
"It Is Written": The Authority of the Bible
Salvation through Jesus Christ: Basics of Forgiveness
Grace, Faith, and Obedience: The Gospel or Calvinism?
Growing a Godly Marriage & Raising Godly Children
The God of the Bible (study of the Father, Son, and Holy Spirit)
"In the Beginning God Created": Creation vs. Evolution
Kingdom of Christ: Future Millennium or Present Spiritual Reign?
Marx, Lenin, or Jesus: Communism or the Bible?
Do Not Sin Against the Child: Abortion, Unborn Life, & the Bible
Short Bible Talks: Invitations, Lord's Supper and Collection Talks

Commentaries on Bible Books

Genesis	*Daniel*	*Galatians*
Joshua and Ruth	*Hosea – Obadiah*	*Ephesians*
Judges	*Gospel of Matthew*	*Philippians &*
1 and 2Samuel	*Gospel of Mark*	*Colossians*
1 and 2 Kings	*Gospel of Luke*	*1 & 2 Thessalonians*
Ezra, Nehemiah, Esther	*Gospel of John*	*Hebrews*
Job	*Acts*	*James and Jude*
Proverbs	*Romans*	*1 and 2 Peter*
Ecclesiastes		*1,2,3 John*

Bible Question Class Books

Genesis	*Daniel*	*2 Corinthians and*
Joshua and Ruth	*Hosea-Obadiah*	*Galatians*
Judges	*Jonah-Zephaniah*	*Ephesians and*
1 and 2 Samuel	*Haggai-Malachi*	*Philippians*
1 and 2 Kings	*Gospel of Matthew*	*Colossians, 1&2*
Ezra/Nehemiah/Esther	*Gospel of Mark*	*Thessalonians*
Job	*Gospel of Luke*	*1 Timothy-Philemon*
Proverbs	*Gospel of John*	*Hebrews*
Ecclesiastes	*Acts*	*James–Jude*
Isaiah	*Romans*	*Revelation*
	1 Corinthians	

Workbooks with Study Notes

Jesus Is Lord: Workbook on the Fundamentals of the Gospel of Christ
Following Jesus: Workbook on Discipleship
God's Eternal Purpose in Christ: Workbook on the Theme of the Bible
Family Reading Booklist

Visit our website at www.gospelway.com/sales to see a current list of books in print.

Other Resources from the Author

Printed books, booklets, and tracts available at
www.gospelway.com/sales
Free Bible study articles online at
www.gospelway.com
Free Bible courses online at
www.biblestudylessons.com
Free class books at
www.biblestudylessons.com/classbooks
Free commentaries on Bible books at
www.biblestudylessons.com/commentary
Contact the author at
www.gospelway.com/comments

Table of Contents

Introductory Notes 9
Part 1: History of Daniel's life 17
Daniel 1 17
Daniel 2 29
Daniel 3 50
Daniel 4 65
Daniel 5 78
Daniel 6 88
Part 2: Daniel's Prophecies 96
Daniel 7 97
Daniel 8 112
Daniel 9 122
Daniel 10 140
Daniel 11 146
Daniel 12 162
Addendum: Applications to Voting 171

(Due to printer reformatting, the above numbers may be off a few pages.)

Notes to the Reader

To save space and for other reasons, I have chosen not to include the Bible text in these notes (please use your Bible to follow along). When I do quote a Scripture, I generally quote the New King James Version, unless otherwise indicated. Often – especially when I do not use quotations marks – I am not quoting any translation but simply paraphrasing the passage in my own words. Also, when I ask the reader to refer to a map, please consult the maps at the back of your Bible or in a Bible dictionary.

You can find study questions to accompany these notes at www.gospelway.com/sales

To join our mailing list to be informed of new books or special sales, contact the author at www.gospelway.com/comments

I want to express thanks to the students in the preachers' Bible study in Columbus for suggestions and comments they offered which have been incorporated in these notes.

Introductory Thoughts about Commentaries

Only the Scriptures provide an infallible, authoritatively inspired revelation of God's will for man (2 Timothy 3:16,17). It follows that this commentary, like all commentaries, was written by an uninspired, fallible human. It is the author's effort to share his insights about God's word for the purpose of instructing and edifying others in the knowledge and wisdom found in Scripture. It is simply another form of teaching, like public preaching, Bible class teaching, etc., except in written form (like tracts, Bible class literature, etc.). Nehemiah 8:8; Ephesians 4:15,16; Romans 15:14; 1 Thessalonians 5:11; Hebrews 3:12-14; 5:12-14; 10:23-25; Romans 10:17; Mark 16:15,16; Acts 8:4; 2 Timothy 2:2,24-26; 4:2-4; 1 Peter 3:15.

It follows that the student must read any commentary with discernment, realizing that any fallible teacher may err, whether he is teaching orally or in writing. So, the student must compare all spiritual teaching to the truth of God's word (Acts 17:11). It may be wise to read several commentaries to consider alternative views on difficult points. But it is especially important to consider the *reasons or evidence* each author gives for his views, then compare them to the Bible.

For these reasons, the author urges the reader to always consider my comments in light of Scripture. Accept what I say only if you find that it harmonizes with God's word. And please do not cite my writings as authority, as though people should accept anything I say as authoritative. Always let the Bible be your authority.

"He who glories, let him glory in the Lord" – 1 Corinthians 1:31

Abbreviations Used in These Notes

ASV – American Standard Version
b/c/v – book, chapter, and verse
ESV – English Standard Version
f – the following verse
ff – the following verses
HCSB – Holman Christian Standard Bible
KJV – King James Version
NASB – New American Standard Bible
NEB – New English Bible
NIV – New International Version
NKJV – New King James Version
NRSV – New Revised Standard Version
RSV – Revised Standard Version

Introductory Notes

Introduction to Old Testament Prophets

The work of prophets

The Old Testament prophets were inspired spokesmen for God. Exodus 4:16, compared to Exodus 7:1, shows that a prophet was a spokesman. Hebrews 1:1 says that God spoke in times past to the fathers by the prophets. 2 Peter 1:21 says that they spoke as they were moved by the Holy Spirit. The prophets often claimed at the beginning of their writings, and sometimes throughout their writings, that they were guided by God in their teaching. They were required to speak exactly the message that God gave them (Deuteronomy 18:19-22).

Prophets sometimes predicted the future, but that was not a necessary part of their work, nor in many cases was it their primary work. Rather, their work was to deliver to people whatever message God gave them by direct guidance of the Holy Spirit.

The prophets did not always teach by the **written** word. Many prophets taught **orally** and never did write down their messages. Some such prophets would include Abraham (Genesis 20:7,17), Miriam (Exodus 15:20), Deborah (Judges 4:4), Elijah and Elisha (1 and 2 Kings), Nathan (2 Samuel 12), and a whole host of other prophets who spoke to the people of Israel during the time of the kings.

The first prophet to write down a message that has been preserved for us was, of course, Moses. But the books that we usually think of as the books of prophecy generally came later in the history of the people of Israel. Those whose books are longer, we have labeled "Major Prophets," and those who are shorter we have labeled "Minor Prophets." The difference has nothing to do with the importance of their message but refers simply to the length of their writings.

Understanding Old Testament prophecy

The Old Testament prophets are a valuable and important part of God's revelation to man. Unfortunately, far too often God's people today tend to neglect studying the prophets. Perhaps some think, because the message was spoken to the Israelites in the Old Testament, that they have no meaning for us today. Or perhaps some think they are too difficult to understand.

Here are some important points to remember when studying Old Testament prophecy.

* ***The prophets are part of Scripture, and all Scripture is profitable to equip us in our service to God today*** – 2 Timothy 3:16,17; Romans 15:4; 1 Corinthians 10:6,11. Even though the prophets spoke to God's people in the Old Testament, their teachings contain many important lessons for us to learn regarding our own service to God, just as is true for other parts of the Old Testament. We should study the prophets looking for lessons and applications for today.

* Because the prophets often refer to kings or events in their own day, ***studying books of Old Testament history may help us understand the background behind the prophets' teachings***. This in turn may help us understand and give a proper interpretation of the message.

* ***The prophets often used parables and other forms of symbolic teaching.*** These may sometimes be difficult to understand, but ***that does not give us the right to assign a meaning to the symbols according to our own fancy or imagination***.

Far too often teachers speculate about prophecy with no substantial evidence to verify their claims. As with all symbols, the goal of the student must be to understand what the inspired writer meant as guided by God. We have no right to assign our own meaning to this teaching other than what God intended. 2 Peter 3:15,16

* ***In particular, the Old Testament prophets often included predictions about the Messiah, His Kingdom, and His message.*** These sometimes appear unexpectedly. The best way to understand when this happens and the meaning of these predictions is by examining New Testament teaching.

Often New Testament writers refer to these Old Testament prophecies and give us an inspired explanation. These may come in the form of direct quotations of Old Testament prophecies or by means of applications or by explanation of other similar prophecies. Prophecy should never be interpreted in a way that contradicts New Testament explanations. Luke 24:25-27; Acts 3:18-26

Introduction to the Book of Daniel

Author

The inspired writer was Daniel (with perhaps editorial notes from some other inspired writer). Daniel frequently referred to himself directly indicating that the message that he wrote was his message. He recorded events that happened to him and visions that he saw (7:15; 8:1,15,27, 9:2; 10:2,7; 12:4,5).

The claims of liberal skeptics

As is to be expected, many liberal skeptics deny that Daniel wrote this book of prophecy, and others deny or doubt that Daniel even existed at all. They claim that the record of his life was invented and written much later than the time period in which the events in the book claim to have occurred. The purpose of such claims is to weaken the power of Daniel's predictions and their subsequent fulfillment.

Bible writers frequently claimed that the fact they could infallibly predict the future proved that they were inspired by God. If Bible writers were able to repeatedly predict future events – events that could not possibly be known by human ability – and if those predictions invariably came true, this would constitute powerful evidence that God exists and that He was speaking through these men just as they claimed that He was. See Isaiah 41:21-23; 42:8,9; 46:8-11; Deuteronomy 18:21,22; Jeremiah 28:9; John 13:19, 14:29; Luke 24:25-27,44-46; John 5:39,46; Acts 2:23-36; 3:18-24; 17:2,3; 10:43; 13:27-39; 26:22,23; 1 Corinthians 15:1-8; 2 Peter 1:19.

In order to combat the power of fulfilled prophecy as evidence for God and for the inspiration of Bible writers, skeptics seek to deny that the writers wrote at the point in history that the Bible says they did. Rather, they claim that these messages were written when the events they claim to predict could be known without miraculous guidance from God.

In Daniel's case, that would mean he must have written during the Roman Empire and after the fall of the Grecian empire, else how could he have predicted the Roman Empire? But no one thinks Daniel wrote that late, so some liberals claim that Daniel did not predict the Roman Empire. They say he predicted two separate empires of the Persians and the Medes, and then the Grecian empire. They say that the book of Daniel was written during the period of the Maccabees; so Daniel wrote history, not prophecy.

Evidence regarding the inspiration of Daniel

Ezekiel 14:14,20 mentions Daniel, listing him as a righteous man along with Noah and Job. Ezekiel 28:3 refers to Daniel as a very wise man. So both as an inspired prophet and as a historian, Ezekiel confirms that Daniel lived, that he lived at the time the Bible claims that he did, and that he was widely known to be a righteous man. Daniel was a real man who lived in history just as Noah and Job did.

In Matthew 24:15 Jesus himself referred to "Daniel the prophet," who prophesied regarding the abomination of desolation at the destruction of Jerusalem (compare Mark 13:14). So Jesus also confirmed that Daniel really lived and that he was a prophet who accurately predicted the future. All the evidence that confirms the inspiration and Deity of Jesus also validates the accuracy and claims of Daniel.

In addition, there is no doubt that the tradition of the Jewish nation accepted the book of Daniel as having been written by Daniel at the very time that the book implies it was written and long before the time of the Maccabees.

So once again liberal skeptics are demonstrated to reject, not just specific historical accounts, but the accuracy and inspiration of Scripture as a whole. And in fact, they deny the trustworthiness of Jesus Christ Himself.

Horne states:

> Of the genuineness and authenticity of the book of Daniel we have every possible evidence, both external and internal.
>
> 1. With regard to the external evidence, we have not only the general testimony of the whole Jewish church and nation, which have constantly received this book as canonical; but we have the particular testimony of Josephus, who (we have seen) commends Daniel as the greatest of prophets; of the Jewish Targums and Taliauds, which frequently quote and appeal to his authority; of Jesus Christ himself, who has cited his words, and has styled him "Daniel the prophet" (compare Daniel ix. 26, 27. with Matthew xxiv. 15. and Mark xiii. 14.); and likewise of the apostle Paul, who has frequently quoted or alluded to him (compare Daniel iii. 23-25. and vii. 22. with Hebrews xi. 33, 34. and Daniel xi. 36. with 2 Thessalonians ii. 4.), as also of St. John, whose Revelation derives great light from being compared with the predictions of Daniel. To these testimonies we may add that of Ezekiel, a contemporary writer, who greatly extols his exemplary piety and singular wisdom (Ezekiel xiv. 14. 20. xxviii. 3.), and also the testimony of antient profane historians, who relate many of the same transactions.

The book of Daniel was included in the Septuagint (LXX) translation, and numerous copies of his book were included among the Dead Sea scrolls. This is powerful confirmation that the book was written and had been recognized as Scripture belonging in the Jewish canon long before the fall of Greece.

The following is quoted from "New Light on the Book of Daniel from the Dead Sea Scrolls," Gerhard Hasel PhD, July 2012;

https://biblearchaeology.org/research/divided-kingdom/3193-new-light-on-the-book-of-daniel-from-the-dead-sea-scrolls?highlight=WyJkYW5pZWwiLCJkYW5pZWwncyJd

> "Inasmuch as Daniel was already canonical at Qumran at about 100 BC, how could it have become so quickly canonical if it had just been produced a mere half century before? ... Both the canonical status and the fact that Daniel was considered a 'prophet' speak for the antiquity of the book of Daniel. An existence of a mere five decades between the production of a

Biblical book in its final form and canonization does not seem reasonable.

> "Thus the canonical acceptance of the book of Daniel at Qumran suggests an earlier origin of the book than the second century BC. In 1969, based on the evidence available at that time regarding the Qumran Daniel texts, Roland K. Harrison had already concluded that the second century dating of the book of Daniel was "absolutely precluded by the evidence from Qumran ... The most recent publications of Daniel manuscripts confirm this conclusion."

Careful studies likewise confirming the above information are found in the introductions written by Archer, Young, and Price (see our bibliography). See also our notes on chapter 2 regarding the identity of the four empires that Daniel predicted and our notes on chapter 3 regarding arguments about the musical instruments named there.

Regarding the apocryphal sections that have been added to the book of Daniel, Horne says:

> In the Vulgate Latin edition of the Bible, ... there is added in the third chapter of Daniel, between the twenty-third and twenty-fourth verses, the song of the three children, Hananiah, Mishael, and Azariah, who were cast into the fiery furnace; and, at the end of the book, the history of Susanna and the story of Bel and the Dragon are inserted as the thirteenth and fourteenth chapters. But these additions were never received into the canon of Holy Writ by the Jewish church; neither are they, extant in the Hebrew or Chaldee languages, nor is there any evidence that they ever were so extant. ... The church of Rome, however, allows these spurious additions to be of the same authority with the rest of the book of Daniel; and, by a decree of the fourth session of the council of Trent, has given them an equal place in the canonical Scriptures. But they were never recognised as part of the sacred volume by the antient fathers of the Christian church. Julius Africanus, Eusebius, and Apollinarius rejected these pieces, not only as being uncanonical, but also as fabulous: and Jerome, who has been followed by Erasmus and other modern writers, has given the history of Bel and the Dragon no better title than that of "The Fables of Bel and the Dragon." ...

Theme

The book of Daniel describes the life and prophecies of Daniel during the captivity of Judah in the Babylonian Empire and later in the Persian Empire. The message frequently emphasizes the rule of God in the kingdoms of men.

A list of the periods of Bible history

The life and prophecies of Daniel need to be placed in their proper perspective in Bible history. We may divide Bible history into the following fifteen periods:

1. **Before the Flood** (from Creation to the flood)
2. **After the Flood** (from the flood to the call of Abraham)
3. **Patriarchs** – the Israelite "fathers" or heads of families (from the call of Abraham to the death of Joseph)
4. **Egyptian Bondage** (from the death of Joseph to the crossing of the Red Sea)
5. **Wilderness Wandering** (from the crossing of the Red Sea to the crossing of the Jordan)
6. **Conquest of Canaan** (from the crossing of the Jordan to the death of Joshua)
7. **Judges** (from the death of Joshua to the crowning of King Saul)
8. **United Kingdom** (from the crowning of King Saul to the death of King Solomon)
9. **Divided Kingdom** (from the death of Solomon to the fall of Israel)
10. **Judah Alone** (from the fall of Israel to the fall of Judah)
11. **Babylonian Captivity** (from the fall of Judah to the first return from captivity)
12. **Restoration of Israel** (from the first return to the completion of the Old Testament)
13. **Years of Silence** (from the completion of the Old Testament to the birth of Jesus)
14. **Life of Christ** (from the birth of Jesus to His ascension)
15. **Early Church** (from Jesus' ascension to the completion of the New Testament)

The life of Daniel pertains to the period of Babylonian captivity. He was taken into captivity in the first group that Nebuchadnezzar and his army carried away to Babylon.

Summary of prophets by period

Period of History	Prophets	
Divided Kingdom	**Israel:** Jonah Amos Hosea	**Judah:** Obadiah (?) Joel (?) Isaiah Micah
Judah Alone	Jeremiah (Lamentations) Zephaniah Nahum Habakkuk (?)	
Babylonian Captivity	Ezekiel Daniel	
Return from Captivity	Haggai Zechariah Malachi	

Historical background

Nearly all the specific Biblical information that we have about Daniel is revealed in the book of Daniel. However, as mentioned earlier in our quotation from Horne, the Jewish historian Josephus confirms many events in the early life of Daniel. The historical records of the Babylonians and the Persians also confirm many of the events regarding the captivity of the Jews.

Because the people of Judah had rebelled against God and become deeply involved in idolatry, God allowed the Babylonians under king Nebuchadnezzar to attack Judah and take captives away to Babylon. This occurred three different times: 606 BC, 597 BC, and 586 BC. In the final attack, Jerusalem and the temple were destroyed.

Here is a summary of dates in which various groups of people were taken into captivity or returned from captivity, identifying some individuals who were included along with the Scriptures that confirm the events.

Event	Date	People Involved	Scriptures
First captivity	605 BC	King Jehoiakim Daniel, Shadrach, Meshach, Abed Nego	Daniel 1:1-7; 2 Chronicles 36:5-8
Second captivity	597 BC	King Jehoiachin Ezekiel	2 Kings 24:8-17; 2 Chronicles 36:9,10
Third captivity	586 BC	King Zedekiah	2 Kings 25:1-7; 2 Chronicles 36:10-21; Jeremiah 52:1-30
First Return	536 BC	Zerubbabel	Ezra, Haggai, Zechariah
Second Return	467 BC	Ezra	Ezra
Third Return	454 BC	Nehemiah	Nehemiah

Daniel was taken captive as a youth by Nebuchadnezzar into Babylon in the first group of captives in 605 B.C. (1:1-6). The period of captivity continued for 70 years as Jeremiah had prophesied. Daniel lived through the period of the Babylonian Empire into the Medo-Persian Empire.

Even though they were in captivity, the Jews were waiting to return to the promised land. The Messiah was still to come through the lineage of Israel as had been promised through the prophets. The Messiah was also to fulfill the promise to the patriarchs – Abraham, Isaac, and Jacob – that one would come who would be their descendant and would bring a blessing on all nations.

During the early life of Daniel, Jeremiah was still prophesying warning the people of Judah to submit to God's will or they would be taken into captivity in Babylon. So the beginning of the record in the book of Daniel overlaps the last years of the record in the book of Jeremiah. Where Jeremiah tells the story from the standpoint of those who remained in Judah, Daniel tells his story in Babylon.

Ezekiel was taken captive in the second group that Nebuchadnezzar took captive from Judah. His record also overlaps that of Daniel, but Ezekiel tells the story from the viewpoint of God's people who were captives in Babylon.

Other than some overlap in their stories, there is no record that Daniel, Jeremiah, or Ezekiel ever met one another personally. Nevertheless, their accounts record the history of this period of captivity.

Daniel was a man of faith and courage. He rose to great prominence under several kings, yet he never compromised God's will. Many lessons can be learned from his life.

Outline of the book

Part 1: History of Daniel's life – chapters 1-6
    Daniel and his friends refused to eat the king's foods – chapter 1
    Daniel interpreted Nebuchadnezzar's dream of an image – chapter 2
    Daniel's friends refused to bow to Nebuchadnezzar's image and were thrown into a fiery furnace – chapter 3
    Nebuchadnezzar learned that God rules in the kingdoms of men – chapter 4
    Daniel interpreted the handwriting on the wall – chapter 5
    Daniel was thrown into a den of lions, because he prayed to God despite the king's decree– chapter 6

Part 2: Daniel's prophecies – chapters 7-12
    Vision of the four beasts – chapter 7
    Vision of the ram and the male goat – chapter 8
    Daniel's confession and the vision of seventy weeks – chapter 9
    Vision in the third year of Cyrus – chapters 10-12

Part 1: History of Daniel's life – Chapters 1-6

Daniel 1

Chapter 1 – Daniel and His Friends Refused to Eat the King's Foods.

Daniel Purposed to Remain Pure

Nebuchadnezzar captured Jerusalem and took to Babylon some articles from the temple.

The king instructed special young men to be given special training and a special diet.

Daniel and his three friends were chosen.

Daniel purposed not to defile himself with the king's delicacies.

Daniel suggested a test in which he and his friends would have their own diet for ten days.

The king found them ten times better than his occult advisors.

1:1,2 – *In the third year of the reign of Jehoiakim, Nebuchadnezzar and the Babylonians besieged Jerusalem. The Lord allowed them to capture Jehoiakim and take some articles from the house of God to Shinar and put them in the treasure house of their own God.*

Nebuchadnezzar took articles from the house of God and put them into the treasure house of his god in Shinar.

Despite the fact that they were God's chosen people, the nation of Judah became increasingly sinful, including the sin of idolatry. This came to a climax with the extreme wickedness of King Manasseh. As a result God predicted that captivity was inevitable (2 Kings 24:1-5), but the captivity was postponed a few generations.

Manasseh's grandson Josiah was one of the best kings that Judah ever had. However, he was slain by Pharaoh Necho at Megiddo, and the people made his son Jehoahaz king (2 Kings 23:28-30). Jehoahaz began to reign when he was twenty-three, but he was wicked. He reigned only three months till Pharaoh Neco took him as a prisoner to Egypt where he died. Pharaoh then made Eliakim, another son of Josiah, king and changed his name to Jehoiakim (2 Kings 23:31-34).

Jehoiakim was twenty-five years old when he began to reign, and he reigned eleven years in Jerusalem. He also did evil in the sight of the Lord (2 Kings 23:36,37). During Jehoiakim's reign, Nebuchadnezzar king of Babylon made him his servant for three years, but then Jehoiakim rebelled. So God allowed Chaldeans and other nations to come against Judah. Nebuchadnezzar carried off parts of the vessels of the house of God (2 Chronicles 36:5-7), and eventually he took Jehoiakim and other Jews as captives to Babylon.

The passage says the Lord gave Jehoiakim into his hand: "The fact that Jehoiakim is recorded to have been given over shows that it was not a victory for the might of his enemies but rather it was of the will of the Lord." – Jerome (*Ancient Christian Commentary*)

Daniel was taken to Babylon along with this first group of captives. This occurred in 606-605 BC. Babylon was at that time the dominant empire of the world, having defeated and overthrown the Assyrian Empire (see a **map**). Their primary opposition in the region of Canaan came from the Egyptians.

The record here in the book of Daniel says that, when Nebuchadnezzar took those articles from the house of God in Jerusalem, he put them in the treasure house of his own God. This would especially be an abomination since the treasures that had been designed to glorify the true God would then be used to glorify a false god.

Babylonian records of these events

The Bible record is substantiated by the histories kept by the Babylonians themselves (although in different language and from a different perspective). The *Archaeology Study Bible* states the following:

> "An incomplete series of cuneiform tablets known as the Babylonian Chronicle ... describes Babylon's victory over Assyria and Egypt at the battle of Carchemish in 605 BC as follows: ... 'the king of Babylon (Nebuchadnezzar's father, Nabopolassar), was in his country (perhaps because of illness or advancing age). Nebuchadnezzar, his eldest son, the crown-prince, mustered the army of Babylon, took command, and marched to Carchemish on the bank of the Euphrates. He crossed the river to face the army of Egypt [and] defeated them utterly...'" (page 1200)
>
> ...
>
> "Nabopolassar died while Nebuchadnezzar was out with the army, so the crown prince raced back to the capital to claim the Babylonian throne. He rejoined the army and swept southward along the eastern Mediterranean, consolidating the new Babylonian gains in the region and taking a great deal of plunder. This included sacred articles from the Israelite temple in Jerusalem as well as Daniel and his three friends." (page 1201)
>
> ...
>
> "The Chronicle also describes Nebuchadnezzar's subjection of Jerusalem in 597 BC: '... The king (Nebuchadnezzar) ... mustered his army and marched to Hattu (the lands along the eastern Mediterranean). He besieged the city of Judah (Jerusalem). ... He took the city and captured the king [Jehoiachin]. He appointed a king of his own choosing – [Zedekiah]." (page 1200)

The above explanation would mean that Nebuchadnezzar had become king before he captured Daniel and his friends. However, some students believe that Nebuchadnezzar was not yet actually king at the time when he captured Daniel and his friends. Yet Daniel's account and also Jeremiah's account refer to him as king. Keil & Delitzsch explain as follows:

> ...the circumstance that Nebuchadnezzar, as stated in Jer 46:2; Jer 25:1, and also Dan 1:1, was called king of Babylon before he had actually ascended the throne is no valid objection, inasmuch as this title is explained as a prolepsis [use of a term which anticipates a later event that everyone understands occurred] which would be easily understood by the Jews in Palestine ... whether on account of his being actual co-regent

with his aged and infirm father, or merely because he was clothed with royal power as the chief commander of the army.

In other words, the reign of a son often overlapped that of his father. In the later years of a king's life, he may appoint his son to reign with him, so they were both spoken of as king. But the son did not actually become king in his own right till the death of the father. Another possibility is that Nebuchadnezzar is spoken of as king because he was acting as commander of the army and eventually did become king in his own right.

When speaking after the fact about someone who everyone knows became a king or president, etc., it is common to refer to them by their title even when describing a time before they actually were in office. So, for example, we might say that President Washington was born in Virginia. Obviously he was not president when he was born, yet we refer to him as president because everyone knows that eventually he became president.

The Bible record is substantially confirmed by the Babylonian record. There is no substantial contradiction, though there may be some questions about exact dates and terminology.

Other questions of dates

Other questions remain regarding the exact order when various events in the records occurred and the number of years involved.

One question relates to the fact that Daniel's account says Nebuchadnezzar besieged Jerusalem in the third year of the reign of Jehoiakim, whereas Jeremiah says it was the fourth year (Jeremiah 25). Such a small difference may simply be a matter of how the years were counted.

Archaeology Study Bible (page 1201) explains that reigns could be numbered in various ways. People in Judah may have counted the years beginning with the first year of the king's reign. But others (including Daniel in Babylon) may not have counted the year in which a king actually came into power but began the numbering with the following year.

Another question relates to the fact that Daniel's account says Nebuchadnezzar besieged Jerusalem in the third year of Jehoiakim, but other accounts say that Jehoiakim reigned for eleven years in Jerusalem. However, Daniel's account does not necessarily mean that Nebuchadnezzar took Jehoiakim captive in the third year of his reign. He may simply have taken some captives at that time along with some articles from the temple. But Jehoiakim himself may have continued to reign a few more years and then have been captured in a later siege.

1:3-5 – Nebuchadnezzar took to Babylon some young men who had wisdom, intelligence, good looks, and other advantages. They were to be educated and trained for three years and fed with the king's delicacies and wine, so they might learn to serve before the king.

Nebuchadnezzar instructed Ashpenaz, the master of his eunuchs, that among the captives from Israel they should bring some who were descendants of the king or otherwise of the nobility. This would include especially young men who were without blemish and good-looking, gifted in wisdom and knowledge and intelligence

These young men would be trained in the language and literature of the Chaldeans so they would be able to serve in the king's palace. They would also be given a special diet which would include a daily provision of the king's delicacies and the wine that he himself drank. This period of training would continue for three years, and at the end of that time they would be qualified to serve before the king.

Apparently Nebuchadnezzar wanted to have servants around him who had special talents and training. He hoped they would serve as wise counselors and able assistants who could use their special talents and intelligence for the good of his administration. This would appear to be good advice even for political leaders today. If a leader gathers around him people who have special training and abilities in the various areas that are needed in order to govern, he would have a better opportunity for successful leadership.

1:6,7 – Daniel, Hananiah, Mishael, and Azariah were included among the captives chosen to be given the special training. The chief of the eunuchs gave Daniel the name Belteshazzar. Then he gave to Hananiah, Mishael, and Azariah the names Shadrach, Meshach, and Abed Nego.

These verses introduce us to Daniel, his friends, and their circumstances. This informs us that they were of the tribe of Judah and were part of the captives that were taken to Babylon by Nebuchadnezzar in the first group of captives. The fact that these young men were included in this group chosen for special training also tells us some other important things about them.

First, they were young men, since that was the kind of men who were chosen. It follows that the lessons we learn, especially in the early parts of the life of Daniel, are important lessons for all of us, but especially for young people. Daniel's life was worthy of imitation in many ways and many important lessons can be learned.

Second, all of these young men possessed special talents and intelligence. Those chosen were of the nobility, good-looking, without blemish, intelligent, and gifted in wisdom. So these were exceptional young men in many ways, but we will see especially that these four men were also very courageous and firm in their dedication to the true God.

We are not told the exact age of the young men at this time. Commentators tend to suspect that they were in their late teens, though this is not conclusive. What is important is the fact that they were mature enough to have demonstrated the qualities that the king was looking for.

But they were also mature enough to have developed a sense of responsibility to stand for what they knew to be right. They had evidently been trained already in the true religion according to the Old Testament law. Being taken to a foreign land, uprooted from their family and country, would have been extremely difficult. But none of these hardships excused them from the responsibility to do right.

The chief of the eunuchs renamed each of these four young men. To Daniel he gave the name Belteshazzar. Then he gave to Hananiah, Mishael, and Azariah the names Shadrach, Meshach, and Abed Nego. The reason for the name change is not stated here, nor are we told the meaning of the names.

Some commentators have concluded that the Jewish names of these young men identified them with the God of Israel, but the Babylonians renamed them in order to free them from that background and tie them instead to Babylon, perhaps especially to the Babylonian gods. The only clue I can find to confirm this is that Nebuchadnezzar later said that he gave the name Belteshazzar to Daniel to name him after Nebuchadnezzar's god (4:8). In any case, it is clear that Daniel attempted throughout the book to continue using his Jewish name.

> "Although the meanings of their new names are not certain, they likely honor Babylonian gods, in contrast to the Hebrew names that honor Yahweh. Daniel ("God is my judge") becomes Belteshazzar ("Lady [wife of Marduk, patron god of Babylon], protect the life of the king!"), Hananiah ("Yahweh is gracious") is changed to Shadrach ("command of Aku [the moon god]), Mishael ("Who is what God is?") is called Meshach ("Who is what Aku is?"), and Azariah ("Yahweh helps") becomes Abednego ("servant of Nego/Nebo/Nabu" [the son of Maduk])."
> – *Archaeology Study Bible*, page 1202

1:8-10 – Daniel requested of the chief eunuch that he not defile himself with the delicacies and wine that the king had appointed. The chief eunuch was favorable toward Daniel, but he was afraid he would be in danger with the king if a different diet hindered Daniel's appearance.

The king had chosen a special diet to be given to these young men who were in training (verses 3-5). However, Daniel determined in his heart that he would not defile himself with the king's delicacies.

For some unstated reason, the food was not lawful. The reason is not stated. Perhaps it had been offered to idols, so eating it was considered worship of the idol. Or it could have been unclean according to the Old Testament law. (Compare Leviticus 11:47; Ezekiel 4:13,14.) Still another possibility was that the meat had not been properly slain, draining the blood in accordance with Old Testament requirements (Leviticus 17:10-16). (Keil & Delitzsch prefer the first explanation, because the second two explanations would not explain why Daniel refused to drink the wine.)

Notice that 10:3 implies that Daniel later ate meat and drank wine. So apparently he did not object to eating meat as such. Whatever problem existed here in chapter 1 was apparently later no longer an issue.

The chief eunuch was favorable towards Daniel and had good will toward him. But he was also aware of the problems that would occur if he changed the diet as Daniel was requesting. The special diet had been assigned by the king himself. If the diet was changed, and if the result hindered Daniel and his friends in their training, then chief eunuch would be in danger with the king himself.

Daniel's decision required firm purpose: resolution.

The circumstances created severe pressure on Daniel and his friends to participate in that which they opposed. It was a great honor to be chosen for this special training. It would have been easy to become proud in this place of preeminence: to desire honor in spite of the sin that may have been involved. But Daniel determined to resist the instructions of the king himself.

Likewise today, many circumstances tempt Christians to defile ourselves. Even as Daniel did, we must refuse to participate in that which defiles us. Often, we defile ourselves because we don't have a firm purpose in our hearts.

On our jobs, for example, we may be asked to lie, cheat, drink alcoholic beverages or provide drinks to entertain clients, or to contribute to unscriptural organizations (such as United Fund). Other employees may use impure language, laugh at off-color jokes, gamble (bet on sports events), attend cocktail parties, dress immodestly, and condone or overlook the immorality of others. We may be tempted to go along with these errors in order to get ahead in our job.

Titus 2:11-14 – We are saved for the **intent** (purpose) of living a righteous, godly life. Jesus gave Himself that we might belong to him and accomplish good works. Like Daniel, we must keep firmly in mind our purpose as followers of Jesus and our reward at His return.

Colossians 3:2-10 – We must set our minds on our goal. We have been separated from the old life of sin, and we have a glorious reward ahead of us. So we must purpose to put to death sinful lusts and remove them from our lives.

Daniel practiced purity from the time of his youth.

Daniel was a youth when chosen to receive a privileged position among the king's servants (verse 4). This involved especially difficult circumstances. These young men were educated, not in the training of God's word, but in the royal schools of Babylonian wisdom. Yet Daniel resisted temptation and remained true to God. Young people today need this same devotion.

Consider some problems people typically face today.

False education

Many young people today face temptations in the education given in modern schools. False teaching is often presented based on human wisdom. This includes:

* Evolution – the false belief that man has developed from lower animals over millions of years

* Situation ethics – the belief that sin is acceptable under certain circumstances

* Materialism – the belief that that the purpose in life is to obtain or enjoy earthly possessions and pleasures

False moral standards

Young people are often influenced by teachers and other students to accept false moral standards. These include:

* "Free love," "safe sex," pornography, and sexually suggestive activities

Some think that sexual activity is not restricted to marriage, so any form of sexual expression is acceptable as long as you "love one another," have a "meaningful relationship," and use "protection." Schools often encourage such thinking by promoting "sex education," dances, lax dress codes, and immodest uniforms for cheerleaders, baton girls, and mixed gym classes.

Pornographic and sexually suggestive activities bombard young people on the Internet, cell phones, computer games, music, television, movies, and other forms of entertainment.

* "Drug culture" and alcohol

People take recreational drugs or alcohol to stimulate excitement, relax, be sociable, have fun, or escape reality. Young people are sometimes pressured to participate in order to prove that they are mature or that they are not "chicken" or "square."

Many today run with the wrong crowd, "sow their wild oats" while young, then want to turn to God in their old age after they have "had their fun."

False purpose in life

Many young people fail to realize, either through ignorance or rebellion, that they were put here for a purpose. Rather than learning the real purpose of life and seeking to pursue it, they seek to please themselves and their friends.

* Over emphasis on pleasure, games, sports, music, entertainment, and physical appearance

These may or may not be sinful in and of themselves, but the temptation is to focus life on fun and a good time while neglecting the far more important purposes of life and service to God.

   * Pleasing friends and peers, following the crowd, popularity, and fashion

Young people are often highly influenced by desire to be part of the group and go along with the crowd. They often are more concerned about what their friends think that they are about honoring their parents or even obeying God. Often they seek to be popular in school and follow the latest fads and fashions, even if those fashions are indecent or immoral.

   * Self-will and rebellion against authority

Many young people are determined to have their own way and live to please themselves in rebellion and disobedience to the authority of parents, government, the Bible, and God. They may be determined to do their own thing, insisting that no one should tell them what to do with their lives. "I want to live like my own way."

Problems Faced by Young People

False education
* Evolution
* Situation ethics
* Materialism

False moral standards
* "Free love," "safe sex," pornography, and sexually suggestive activities
* "Drug culture" and alcohol

False purpose in life
* Over emphasis on pleasure, games, sports, music, entertainment, and physical appearance
* Pleasing friends and peers, following the crowd, popularity, and fashion
* Self-will and rebellion against authority

To remain pure in such a society, like Daniel, young people need a firm purpose.

Note Ecclesiastes chap 12.

> **To Remain Pure, Young People Must Remember the Following** (Ecclesiastes 12)
>
> * *Remember your origin: Where did I come from?* "Remember also you Creator in the days of you youth..." (Ecclesiastes 12:1). You did not get here by a natural process of evolution. You were **made** by the all-powerful, all wise Ruler of the universe.
>
> * *Remember your purpose: Why am I here?* "Fear God and keep His commandments; for this is the whole duty of man" (Ecclesiastes 12:13). The God who created you put you here for the purpose of serving Him and obeying His will.
>
> * *Remember your destiny: Where am I going?* "God will bring every work into judgment, with every hidden thing, whether it be good, or whether it be bad" (Ecclesiastes 12:14). You will give account for your life. As a result you will receive a destiny of eternal life or eternal punishment.

Like Daniel, young people need to understand the meaning of life and purpose to remain pure in their service to their Creator.

1:11-13 – Daniel asked the steward to test Daniel and his friends for ten days by giving them vegetables to eat and water to drink. Then he could compare them to those who ate the king's delicacies and see which diet accomplished the most good.

Note the method Daniel used to solve the problem.

He called the steward who was in charge of his diet and proposed a test. He requested that he and his three friends be fed vegetables to eat and water to drink for ten days. Then the steward could examine their appearance and compare them to those who remained on the diet the king had commanded. This should help demonstrate whether the diet Daniel suggested was in any way endangering the king's command.

We are not told the specifics of what was involved in the diet the king had instructed. So as already discussed, we do not really know why Daniel objected to it. Whatever that diet involved, Daniel was convinced that vegetables and water would be an improvement.

The passage should not be used to argue that people should be vegetarians and avoid eating meat. The Old Testament had restrictions on unclean meats, but neither the Old Testament nor the New Testament forbade eating meat, nor did they require eating only vegetables or drinking only water. Such a diet may be acceptable for those who choose it, but it is not required by Scripture. As already mentioned, Daniel 10:3 implies that Daniel himself ate meat on other occasions.

See Genesis 9:1-6; 18:2,7,8; Exodus 12:3,6,8,46; 3:8,17; 13:5; 33:3; Leviticus 20:24; 11:2,3,9,21,46,47; 17:13,14; Deuteronomy 27:3;

12:15,20-22; 1 Kings 17:4,6; Proverbs 27:23-27; Jeremiah 32:22; Acts 10:9-16; 11:5-10; 1 Timothy 4:1-5; 1 Corinthians 8:8,10,13; 10:25; Colossians 2:16; Luke 5:4-10; 11:11-13; 15:23,27; 24:36-43; Mark 6:35-44; 8:1-9; 7:18,19; 14:12,18; John 21:3,6,8-13.

Consider the wisdom in Daniel's approach.

(1) He was respectful to those in authority. He did not just rebel and refuse to cooperate. He knew the steward had a responsibility, so he tried to reason with him. He did not complain to everybody else, but went straight to the one in charge and worked the problem out with him.

This is an important lesson for us as well. Often people who disagree with a decision made by those in authority will fuss and complain to everyone except the person responsible. Such an approach spreads discontent and disrespect for those in authority. The one in charge is the one who can solve the problem, so why not talk to that person?

Other people will go to the one in authority but with a rebellious, mean-spirited attitude. Rather than recognizing that the person has authority and that they themselves should seek to submit to that authority, they approach the person so disrespectfully that they are wrong in their manner even if they are correct in their view of the specific decision that was made.

(2) He did not just object to the situation, he suggested a **remedy**. He worked to find a mutually acceptable solution. One mistake I have often made in my life – which no doubt other people have also made – is complaining about the things that other people do, criticizing and faultfinding, without offering helpful suggestions to improve the situation.

It is one thing to criticize a problem, but it is another thing to find a way to solve the problem. Too often we find ourselves being critics rather than being helpful.

1:14-16 – The steward agreed to the test. At the end of ten days Daniel and his friends looked better than those who ate the king's delicacies. So the steward changed the diet, removed the delicacies and wine, and instead gave Daniel and his friends vegetables.

The steward agreed to try the test for ten days as Daniel had suggested. The test was successful: Daniel and his friends looked better in countenance and flesh than those who had been on the diet the king and recommended. So Daniel and his friends were allowed from then on to continue their own diet.

Again, we do not know what the problem was with the king's diet. Nor do we really know why the test proved successful. Outward appearance is not always the proof of a good diet. It could be that God intervened specifically on behalf of Daniel and his friends, blessing them because they had chosen to follow His will rather than following the king's instructions.

In any case, the test was successful so that Daniel and his friends were able to avoid the problems that troubled them. Many times (though not always) we will find that the difficulties that we face can be resolved if we approach them with wisdom and patience and if we are determined to obey God and trust Him to care for us.

1:17-19 – God gave knowledge and wisdom to Daniel and his friends, and Daniel had understanding in visions and dreams. At the end of the three years of testing, they were brought before the king to be interviewed. None were found as good as Daniel and his friends, so they served before the king.

The training period for these young people was to last three years (verse 5). During that time, God blessed the development of Daniel and his three friends. He gave them knowledge, wisdom, and skill in literature. In particular, Daniel was given understanding in visions and dreams. We will see the significance of Daniel's ability in dreams as the story of his life proceeds.

At the end of the training period, the chief of the eunuchs brought the various men before king Nebuchadnezzar to be interviewed. As a result, none was found as acceptable and pleasing to the king as Daniel and his friends. So they served before the king.

Notice the passage expressly says that this wisdom, knowledge, and ability was given to these young men by God. The training given by the schools of the Babylonians may have had some benefit, but these young men trusted in God and God blessed them with the skills that they needed. In particular, we will see in the next chapter that Daniel's ability to interpret dreams involved direct revelation from God. Daniel was a prophet and later received prophecies we will study in this book.

People today do not receive direct revelation, because it is no longer needed. We have all the guidance and instruction that we need revealed in the written Scriptures, which are now complete and contain all truth. Nevertheless, true wisdom still comes from God. We need to learn to trust His revelation as the source of true meaning in life (see Proverbs 1:7; 2 Timothy 3:15-17).

1:20,21 – In all matters of wisdom and understanding in which the king examined Daniel and his friends, he found them ten times better than all the magicians and astrologers in his realm. So Daniel continued to serve even into the time of king Cyrus in the Persian Empire.

Daniel had remained true to his faith in God, trusting in God rather than in human wisdom. So, God blessed him and his friends with wisdom ten times greater than all the other advisors the king had. This describes the outcome of the time of training, but it appears also to describe the role in general that Daniel and his friends had in the service of the king.

Note that these advisors were magicians and astrologers. Magic and astrology were extremely influential in Babylon. Many kings used such men as advisors, considering them to be helpful in giving guidance and even prediction of the future. We will learn from this book much about these occult practices and how they are inferior to God's revelation.

The present account ends by telling us that Daniel continued until the first year of King Cyrus. Cyrus was a Persian king. The passage does not say that Daniel's service ended in the first year of Cyrus. The point is simply to tell us that Daniel's service continued throughout the period of the Babylonian kings. What happened after that is not discussed here, but some information will be provided later.

Daniel 2

Chapter 2 – Daniel Interpreted Nebuchadnezzar's Dream of the Image.

Nebuchadnezzar's Dream of an Image
King Nebuchadnezzar had a dream and asked his occult advisors to tell the meaning.
The advisors had to tell the dream as well as the interpretation.
All the advisors would be slain if they could not reveal the dream.
Daniel prayed to God, and God revealed the dream and its meaning.
The dream showed an image with a head of gold, chest and arms of silver, belly and thighs of bronze, and legs of iron mixed with clay. A stone made without hands struck the image and crushed it, then the stone filled the earth.
The head of gold was Babylon, the silver represented Persia, the bronze represented Greece, and the legs of iron with clay represented the Roman Empire.
During the last Empire God would set up a kingdom that would consume all those kingdoms and last forever.

2:1-30 - Nebuchadnezzar Had a Dream for Which He Sought the Meaning.

2:1,2 – In the second year of his reign, Nebuchadnezzar had a dream that troubled him deeply. He called upon his magicians, astrologers, sorcerers, and Chaldeans to tell him the dream.

The event recorded here took place in the second year of the reign of Nebuchadnezzar.

However, this creates some difficulty with the fact that Daniel's period of training took three years. If the events in chapter 2 took place in Nebuchadnezzar's second year, and these events resulted in Daniel's being exalted above the other magicians, then how could Daniel have been in training three years? Consider some possible explanations.

Keil & Delitzsch appear to believe that Daniel was actually sent to Babylon during the reign of Nabopolassar, so his period of training began before Nebuchadnezzar actually came to the throne. In that case Daniel's three-year training would have ended before Nebuchadnezzar's second year of reign. Then shortly after the end of the training period, the events of chapter 2 would have occurred.

The Waldrons, however, hold the view that Daniel and his friends were sent to Babylon and began their training around the same time that Nebuchadnezzar came to the throne. In that case, the events in chapter 2 would have occurred in the middle of their training. They suppose that Nebuchadnezzar was well pleased with them, as described in chapter 2, but they continued their training and were actually given power at the end of their training. Or perhaps their training ended as result of the events in chapter 2 so they were immediately promoted. (This latter view may not fit well with 1:18; however, perhaps the events in chapter 2 caused the days of training to be interrupted and to end before the three years were expired.)

Another view, which Hailey summarizes based on Young's commentary, is that it is simply a different method of counting time. Jews counted portions of years as being years, but the Babylonians may have counted only complete years when describing the reigns of kings. So, if the training period actually included a portion of a calendar year, then a full year, then another portion, the Jews would have said it was a three-year period. But if Nebuchadnezzar's reign likewise began in the middle of a calendar year, the Babylonians would not have begun counting his reign till the next year, which would have been the first full year of his reign. The training period would then have ended during the second full year of his reign, as stated here in Daniel chapter 2.

Nebuchadnezzar had a dream and called all his wise men to tell him about the dream.

Nebuchadnezzar had a dream that upset or troubled him so that he could not sleep. He called for his various advisors to explain to him the meaning of the dream.

The king's advisors here are called magicians, astrologers, sorcerers, and Chaldeans. While I am not sure of the distinctions in meaning among these terms, the important thing is that they were all involved in occult practices. Babylon was known for its involvement in astrology and other aspects of the occult.

The occult refers to those who seek supernatural information from sources other than the God of the Bible in order either to predict the future or to give advice. The sources of their information may have been idols, demons, Satan himself, dead people, or in some cases the source may not have been clearly known even to the occult practitioner.

Those who use these methods may be referred to as wizards, magicians, mediums, psychics, astrologers, necromancers, or sorcerers. The methods they used may have involved consulting the stars (astrology), palm reading, consulting tea leaves, the Ouija board, consulting the dead, or various incantations and rituals. But regardless of the sources or the methods used, they were all strictly forbidden by God for His people to consult because they were not sources by which He reveals His will.

Unfortunately, as our modern society departs further and further from God and the Bible, people are becoming more and more interested and involved in such occult methods as these. The New Age movement attempts to combine these aspects of the occult with various oriental religions.

So, while I am not completely sure exactly what aspects of the occult Nebuchadnezzar's advisors practiced, we will see as the story proceeds that their occult methods completely failed in providing correct supernatural information. Daniel succeeded by relying on revelation from God.

For passages in which God's word warns us to avoid occult practices, see verse 27.

2:3-6 – The Chaldeans told the king they could interpret the dream if he told it to them. He replied that they must make known the dream and the interpretation. If they did, they would have great rewards; but if not, they and their houses would be destroyed.

Nebuchadnezzar told his occult advisors that he had a dream and was anxious to know the meaning of it. They offered to give the interpretation if he would tell them the dream. But he insisted that they must tell him both the dream and the interpretation. If they could tell him the dream and its meaning, he would give them great gifts, rewards, and honor. But if not, they would be cut to pieces and their houses made an ash heap.

It appears that Nebuchadnezzar could not even remember the dream ("the thing is gone from me" – KJV, ASV). However, some commentators believe that he did remember but refused to tell the dream to his advisers. In any case, if the men were able to give an accurate interpretation of the dream, it is reasonable to expect they could also tell what the dream itself was.

Anyone can make up an interpretation when someone tells them a dream. But telling what the dream was when one has absolutely no clues is essentially impossible. So Nebuchadnezzar's test to his advisers was that, if they had the wisdom to tell him a trustworthy interpretation, they should first prove their ability by telling them what the dream was.

2:7-9 – The Chaldeans again said they would interpret the dream if the king would tell it to them. But Nebuchadnezzar said if they did not make known the dream, then he would know they were just lying. But if they told him the dream, he would know they could interpret it.

Now the Chaldeans were in a real bind. Such people can pretend to have powers when it is relatively easy to make something up and no one can prove they are wrong. But when they are required to do something that demonstrates truly supernatural power, they are stumped. So, they attempted once again to get the king to tell them the dream so they could offer an interpretation.

But Nebuchadnezzar said they were just stalling for time. His decision was firm, and if they did not make known the dream then he would know that they were frauds who were simply lying to him. But if they told him the dream then he would also know that they could give an accurate interpretation.

The expression "till the time has changed" is translated "the situation has changed" (NASB). Perhaps what he meant was that the Chaldeans hoped, if they stalled long enough, he might change his mind or something else might happen that would enable them to escape.

2:10-12 – The Chaldeans said no man on earth could do as the king demanded, and no king had ever before made such a request. No one could do what the king required except the gods who do not make themselves known among men. So, the king was angry and commanded to destroy all the wise men.

The Chaldeans responded that nobody on earth could do what the king was requesting. It was something no king had ever before asked any magician, astrologer, or Chaldean to do. It was so difficult that such information could be revealed only by gods such as did not dwell among men. I suspect this last expression meant that they did not know of any god among them who had the power.

Of course, Nebuchadnezzar's request was reasonable if the men really had the power that they professed to have. If they had supernatural power to interpret dreams, why did they not know how to reveal the dreams in the first place? So, the king became angry and commanded the destruction of all the wise men of Babylon.

The Chaldeans were correct in saying that such knowledge would be available only to a god, and they did not know of any such god. In admitting this, however, they were also acknowledging their own lack of power. They professed to have supernatural power, but when given a truly substantial test of that power, they came up lacking.

They did not know a god who could do such a thing, but that did not prove that there was no such God. It just proved their own limitations.

2:13-16 – The decree went out to begin killing the wise men, which would include Daniel and his companions. When the king's captain Arioch explained the situation, Daniel asked the king for more time so he might reveal the interpretation of the dream.

The king's decree to kill all the wise men in Babylon would also result in the death of Daniel and his three companions. So once again Daniel showed great wisdom and went to one who had power and authority – in this case Arioch, the king's guard. He asked what was the cause of this urgent decree from the king. So Arioch explained to him the situation.

Daniel then requested the king to give him more time. This was apparently the first Daniel had heard of the situation, so he needed to ask God to reveal the information to interpret the king's dream.

2:17-19 – Daniel then explained the decision to his three companions so they would ask God about this secret. Then in a night vision the secret was revealed to Daniel, so he spoke a blessing to God.

Daniel and his friends then asked God to reveal this secret.

Having learned about the decree and the consequences to himself and his companions, Daniel went home to explain the situation to his three friends, Hananiah, Mishael, and Azariah. All four of them then sought God's mercy that He might reveal the secret to them so that they might not die with the other wise men.

God responded to their request by revealing the information in a vision at night to Daniel. A vision was simply a revelation which comes in the form of something seen by the one who receives the revelation. Such methods of revelation were used in various places in Scripture, including several times in the book of Daniel. Peter had such a vision in Acts 10 regarding the need to preach the gospel to the Gentiles.

The fact the vision here occurred at night does not necessarily mean that Daniel was asleep at the time, since Bible accounts of visions generally imply that the one who sees a vision is awake but perhaps in a trance of some kind.

Daniel then offered praise to God for having met their need.

God gives true revelation which cannot be known by any occult power or any other such source.

The Chaldeans had correctly concluded that no God that they knew could provide such information. The situation here defines for us the meaning of a true miracle: an event truly impossible by natural law that could take place only by the power of God. In this case the miracle involved a direct revelation from God.

Furthermore, the situation clearly demonstrates the true miracle power of the true God as compared to fake power of those who falsely claim to have supernatural power. The nature of true miracles is always such that they cannot be truly and consistently duplicated by those who do not have the power of God. The result confirms that a message or truth really comes from God or that the one(s) through whom the message came is truly God's inspired spokesmen, so people can distinguish divine revelation from that which is false.

The Bible contains many other similar examples. Here are few of them: Acts 8:5-13; 13:6-12; Exodus 8:17-19; 1 Kings 18:20-40; Acts 19:11-17.

Note furthermore that those who had the true power of divine revelation and supernatural miracles from God were not afraid or unwilling for their power to be tested in contrast to the fakes and frauds. The very contrast proved who really had a message from God and who did not.

Divine wisdom today is revealed for us in the Scriptures.

1 Corinthians 2:10-13 – Inspired men received knowledge of God's wisdom by the power of the Holy Spirit. They spoke in **words** given by the Holy Spirit.

1 Corinthians 14:37 – These men also **wrote** the inspired message that they received so that what they wrote was "the commandment of the Lord."

2 Peter 1:21 – Prophecy never came by the will of man, but holy men of God spoke as they were moved by the Holy Spirit.

2 Timothy 3:16,7 – All Scripture is given by inspiration of God, and is profitable for doctrine, for reproof, for correction, for instruction in righteousness, that the man of God may be complete, thoroughly equipped for every good work.

When God's instructions for men had been completely revealed and recorded in writing, the gift of direct revelation was no longer needed, so it ceased (1 Corinthians 13:8-13). The power to receive messages from God by direct revelation no longer exists because it completed its purpose when the Bible was completed.

Yet God is still the source of wisdom. Today we have the completed revelation of God recorded for us in Scripture. This is our source of information, and we know it to be true because of the eyewitness testimony of the fulfilled prophecies, miracles, and the resurrection of Jesus.

We do not have direct revelation today, nor do we have the power of divine inspiration to speak to us by dreams. Such power is not needed because we have the Scriptures. Nevertheless, Christians still need to trust God for true wisdom in our lives.

Proverbs 1:7 – "The fear of Jehovah is the beginning of knowledge." As long as we think men are the ultimate source of wisdom, we will never be truly wise.

Proverbs 3:5,6 – When we cease leaning on our thoughts and put our trust in God's wisdom, we receive proper directions for life.

When we send our children off to be educated at schools, universities, etc., are they taught true wisdom? Human learning can be useful in some areas, but in the most important areas of life that pertain to service to God and eternal life, human wisdom is inadequate and often harmful. We need God's wisdom.

The only ultimate source of God's wisdom regarding eternal life today is Scripture: the written Word.

Here are other passages showing the importance of going to the proper source for truth and wisdom: Proverbs 14:12; 26:12; Isaiah 5:21; 47:10; 55:8,9; 65:2; Jeremiah 10:23; 8:9; Acts 17:21; Romans 1:22; 1 Corinthians 1:18-25; 3:19; 2 Corinthians 10:5; Colossians 2:8; 1 Timothy 6:20; 2 Timothy 3:7.

2:20-23 – Daniel praised God for His wisdom and might. God changes times and seasons, removes and raises up kings, and gives wisdom and knowledge. He reveals deep and secret things and knows what is in the darkness. Daniel praised Him for making known what the king demanded.

Daniel then gave God glory for revealing the information that he had requested about the king's dream. We need to remember to express appreciation for the great gifts that God gives us. When we face problems and hardships, we often go to God in prayer and make our requests. We should be just as diligent to give Him thanks when He provides what we need. See Philippians 4:6,7.

Daniel praised God as the ultimate possessor of wisdom and might. Because of His wisdom, God is able to reveal wisdom and knowledge. Those who seek to possess true wisdom and knowledge need to recognize that God is the source. He is the giver of what we need.

God can even reveal that which is secret and unknown. It is as though He is the source of light and can understand all that is dark and otherwise unknowable. For all these reasons, God is able to reveal information like that which Daniel had requested about the king's dream.

Daniel also added that God changes times and seasons, and He removes or raises up kings. The idea of changing times and seasons indicates that God has the power to influence when various events will occur. He can determine what kings will come to power, when they come to power, and when they cease to rule. This further expresses the greatness of God's wisdom and power.

The significance of Daniel's praise to God does relate to the dream that Nebuchadnezzar had. In that dream we will see that God will do through future generations exactly what Daniel here describes. He will influence and change when kingdoms arise, what kings come to power and when they come to power, and He will determine when those kingdoms fall. The dream expresses God's power in the kingdoms of men and how God controls the affairs of mankind.

"[God] often permits wicked kings to arise that they may in their wickedness punish the wicked." – Jerome (*Ancient Christian Commentary*)

2:24-26 – Daniel urged Arioch not to destroy the wise men but to take Daniel before the king. So Arioch took Daniel to the king, and the king asked if Daniel was able to make known his dream and its interpretation.

Since God had revealed the dream and its meaning, Daniel went to Arioch, the man who was responsible for obeying the king's command to slay the wise men of Babylon. He urged him not to destroy the wise men. He said, if he was taken to the king, he would meet the king's demand to give the interpretation of the dream.

So Arioch quickly took Daniel to the king and told him that he had found a man among the captives from Judah who could make known the interpretation of the dream. When Daniel was brought before king Nebuchadnezzar, the king asked if he was able to make known the dream and then reveal the interpretation.

2:27-30 – Daniel said the wise men, astrologers, etc., could not declare the secret. But the true God in heaven reveals secrets, and He had made known a message to the king about the latter days. It was revealed to Daniel, not because of his own greatness, but to send a message to the king.

Before revealing the dream and its meaning, Daniel explained to the king the source of his understanding.

The failure of the occult

Daniel first explained that the various occult sources of information – the magicians, soothsayers, astrologers, etc. – could not reveal the information the king wanted. We have already seen that they were not able to reveal the dream to Nebuchadnezzar and so could not give a reliable interpretation.

The Bible repeatedly shows that occult methods are inferior to the superior power of those inspired men who spoke by the direct guidance of the Holy Spirit. Furthermore, God expressly forbids his people to be involved in the occult, because it is an appeal to spirit forces other than the true God to obtain supernatural information or powers.

Consider other passages that forbid consulting occult powers:

Danger of the Occult

Deuteronomy 18:9-14 – There shall not be found among you anyone who makes his son or his daughter pass through the fire, or one who practices witchcraft, or a soothsayer, or one who interprets omens, or a sorcerer, or one who conjures spells, or a medium, or a spiritist, or one who calls up the dead. For all who do these things are an abomination to the LORD, and because of these abominations the LORD your God drives them out from before you. You shall be blameless before the LORD your God. For these nations which you will dispossess listened to soothsayers and diviners; but as for you, the LORD your God has not appointed such for you.

Leviticus 19:31 – Give no regard to mediums and familiar spirits; do not seek after them, to be defiled by them: I am the LORD your God.

Leviticus 20:6 – And the person who turns to mediums and familiar spirits, to prostitute himself with them, I will set My face against that person and cut him off from his people.

Leviticus 20:27 – A man or a woman who is a medium, or who has familiar spirits, shall surely be put to death; they shall stone them with stones. Their blood shall be upon them.

Isaiah 8:19,20 – And when they say to you, "Seek those who are mediums and wizards, who whisper and mutter," should not a people seek their God? Should they seek the dead on behalf of the living? To the law and to the testimony! If they do not speak according to this word, it is because there is no light in them.

Revelation 22:15 – But outside are dogs and sorcerers and sexually immoral and murderers and idolaters, and whoever loves and practices a lie.

Acts 8:9-13 – But there was a certain man called Simon, who previously practiced sorcery in the city and astonished the people of Samaria, claiming that he was someone great, to whom they all gave heed, from the least to the greatest, saying, "This man is the great power of God." And they heeded him because he had astonished them with his sorceries for a long time. But when they believed Philip as he preached the things concerning the kingdom of God and the name of Jesus Christ, both men and women were baptized. Then Simon himself also believed; and when he was baptized he continued with Philip, and was amazed, seeing the miracles and signs which were done.

> Acts 19:18,19 – And many who had believed came confessing and telling their deeds. Also, many of those who had practiced magic brought their books together and burned them in the sight of all. And they counted up the value of them, and it totaled fifty thousand pieces of silver.
>
> Acts 13:6-12 – Now when they had gone through the island to Paphos, they found a certain sorcerer, a false prophet, a Jew whose name was Bar-Jesus, who was with the proconsul, Sergius Paulus, an intelligent man. This man called for Barnabas and Saul and sought to hear the word of God. But Elymas the sorcerer (for so his name is translated) withstood them, seeking to turn the proconsul away from the faith. Then Saul, who also is called Paul, filled with the Holy Spirit, looked intently at him and said, "O full of all deceit and all fraud, you son of the devil, you enemy of all righteousness, will you not cease perverting the straight ways of the Lord? And now, indeed, the hand of the Lord is upon you, and you shall be blind, not seeing the sun for a time." And immediately a dark mist fell on him, and he went around seeking someone to lead him by the hand. Then the proconsul believed, when he saw what had been done, being astonished at the teaching of the Lord.

Glory belongs to God.

Daniel gave God the thanks and the glory for the wisdom. He did not take credit to himself, but he acknowledged God as the source. He expressed thanks to God for the revelation (verse 23). Before Nebuchadnezzar he gave God the credit as the source of wisdom and knowledge (verses 27-29). He denied that he knew the information because he himself was so wise (verse 30).

Today, when we teach something we know people will not like, we put the responsibility on God's Word. We say, "This isn't my decision. I am just telling you what God's word says." So, when people appreciate the message, let us also remember to give God's Word the credit.

Galatians. 1:11,12 – Paul gave God the credit for the truth he knew and taught.

Psalm 119:7 – The Psalmist gave thanks when he learned God's righteous judgments.

Psalm 119:62 – We should rise and give thanks because of His righteous ordinances.

How often do we think to praise God because He has blessed us with the knowledge of the revelation of His will?

Daniel explained that God sent the dream to reveal the message to the king.

He explained that Nebuchadnezzar had a dream because God was making known to him what would happen in the future. And he had given the meaning of the dream to Daniel so that the king could understand the message.

Daniel here refers to the future as "the latter days" (verse 28). Such a term could simply be a general expression for the future, however it is also a term commonly used in Old Testament prophecies to refer to the period of the New Testament. It was so used in Isaiah 2:2-4; Micah 4:1-4; Joel 2:28. Peter expressly explained that this latter passage was fulfilled in the New Testament or the gospel age. Similar uses are found in other places: see Jeremiah 23:20; 30:24; Ezekiel 38:16; Hosea 3:5; Acts 2:17; Hebrews 1:1,2; 9:26; 1 Peter 1:20; 2 Peter 3:3; 1 John 2:18; Genesis 49:1; Numbers 24:14; Deuteronomy 4:30; Daniel 10:14

2:31-49 - Daniel Revealed the Dream and Its Meaning.

2:31-35 – Nebuchadnezzar saw an image with a head of gold, chest and arms of silver, belly and thighs of bronze, and legs of iron and feet partly iron and partly clay. A stone cut without hands struck the image on its feet so the entire image was crushed to chaff carried away by the wind, but the stone became a great mountain that filled the earth.

These verses state the dream. Nebuchadnezzar saw a great image, excellent in splendor and awesome in form. It was like a man made of different metals as follows:

* A head of gold
* Chest and arms of silver
* Belly and thighs of bronze
* Legs of iron and feet partly iron and partly clay

A stone was cut without hands and struck the image on its feet and broke them in pieces. The entire image – iron, clay, bronze, silver, and gold – was crushed and became like chaff carried away by the wind so no trace was found. But the stone became a great mountain that filled the earth.

This was the dream that Nebuchadnezzar had not been able to remember. But Daniel explains the interpretation in the following verses.

2:36-39 – Daniel's interpretation said that God had given a kingdom to Nebuchadnezzar. He was the head of gold. After him would arise another inferior kingdom, then a third kingdom of bronze which would rule over all the earth.

Having stated the dream, Daniel then proceeded to explain its interpretation to the king.

The image had a head of gold (verse 32). Daniel said this referred to Nebuchadnezzar as the head of gold. But since he proceeded to explain that the other parts of the image referred to kingdoms (verse 39), it follows that the reference was, not to Nebuchadnezzar himself, but to the kingdom of Nebuchadnezzar, that is Babylon (verses 37,38).

Daniel described Nebuchadnezzar's kingdom, saying that he was a king of kings – that is, he ruled over other rulers (compare Ezekiel 26:7; see also Jeremiah 27:5-7). This power was given to him by God as a kingdom with power, strength, and glory (see also chapter 4). Nebuchadnezzar had authority wherever people, animals, or birds would dwell. God had put all this under Nebuchadnezzar's hand so that he ruled it all.

Then the image had a breast and arms of silver (verse 32). Daniel said this would be another kingdom that would arise after Nebuchadnezzar's and would be inferior to his. Notice that the various parts of the image referred to kingdoms. This second kingdom is not named, but we will see that it is clearly identified as the Persian kingdom (verse 39).

Then the image had a belly and thighs of brass or bronze (verse 32). Daniel said this would be a third kingdom which would rule over all the world (verse 39). Note that these are kingdoms that rule all the earth: that is they were worldwide. We call them "empires." Furthermore, they are numbered in succession. This makes the identification of them in history easy.

Historically, the empire of Babylon was followed by three great world empires. Babylon was the first empire, represented by the head of gold. The one that followed was the kingdom of Persia or the Medes and Persians. Some have attempted to separate the Medes and Persians into two separate empires in order to avoid the clear reference to the Roman Empire as the fourth empire. But Daniel clearly identifies the Medes and Persians together as one empire.

> **Evidence that the Medes and Persians Refers to One Combined Empire, Not Two**
>
> Daniel 2:39 – The four kingdoms described in the dream each ruled over all the earth. But the Medes never had a kingdom that ruled over the world as a major empire comparable to Babylon, Assyria, or Greece. The only worldwide kingdom which they controlled was a kingdom consisting of Medes and Persians.
>
> Daniel 5:28 – By inspiration Daniel told Belshazzar that his kingdom would be divided and given to the Medes and Persians. One empire overthrew the Babylonians, and that was a combined empire of Medes and Persians.
>
> Daniel 6:8,12,15 – Daniel lived into the beginning of the Medo-Persian Empire. Several times the law of that empire is referred to as the law of the Medes and Persians. So these were not two separate kingdoms in succession, but the same kingdom having the same law.
>
> Daniel 8:20,21 – In this vision Daniel saw a ram that had two horns, which are specifically said to be the kings of Media and Persia. Following this was a goat which is specifically said to be the king of Greece. As in chapter 7, each of the animals represents a separate kingdom. So the ram represents one kingdom – the Medo Persian Empire – not two separate kingdoms.
>
> Historically, there was no empire of Medes separate from the Persian Empire at this time. The only ones who claim there was a separate empire are liberals who do not respect the infallible inspiration of Scripture. So they attempt to avoid the conclusion that Daniel predicted the Roman Empire, since he could only have done this by inspiration.
>
> This confirms that the second and third empires in Daniel 2 are the Medo Persian Empire and the Greek Empire. Therefore, the fourth empire must be the Roman Empire.

The third great world empire was that of the Greeks or Macedonia.

"Then the Greeks had the supremacy, beginning with Alexander the Macedonian, for three hundred years, so that they were brass." – Hippolytus (*Ancient Christian Commentary*)

These identifications are certain because Daniel said they were empires that "ruled over all the earth," and he numbered them. This information is essential to proper understanding of the dream. These kingdoms were not local nations or city-states but worldwide empires. And there were exactly four of them. This will likewise make the identification of the fourth empire clear.

2:40-43 – The fourth kingdom would be strong as iron. But the feet and toes, partly of clay and partly of iron, showed the kingdom would be divided. It would have the strength of iron, but would also be fragile like iron that does not mix with clay.

The fourth kingdom was represented by the legs of iron and feet of iron mixed with clay (verse 33). This fourth kingdom would be as strong as iron, having the strength of iron to break and shatter and crush, so that it would break in pieces and crush the other kingdoms.

However, as symbolized by the feet and toes of potter's clay mixed with iron, so the kingdom would be divided. It would have the strength of iron in it, but iron does not mingle with clay. So, the mixture of iron and clay in the feet and toes represents the fact the kingdom would be divided. While it had strength, it would also be fragile.

The people of this kingdom would be a mixture of various peoples, but they would not adhere to one another like iron does not mix with clay. They would mingle with the seed of men but would not cleave to one another (ASV). They would mix with one another in marriage, but would not hold together (ESV).

Clearly this is the Roman Empire. This identification is also certain, as it was with the second and third kingdoms. Remember, these are worldwide kingdoms or empires, and they are specifically numbered. Since this is the fourth worldwide kingdom, it must refer to the Roman Empire.

> "Now the fourth empire, which clearly refers to the Romans, is the iron empire that breaks in pieces and overcomes all others. But its feet and toes are partly iron and partly of earthenware … For just as there was at the first nothing stronger or hardier than the Roman realm, so also in these last days there is nothing more feeble…" – Jerome (*Ancient Christian Commentary*)

The identification of these empires is generally accepted among those who accept the Bible as the inspired word of God (generally only liberal skeptics, who seek to undermine the inspiration of Daniel, dispute this conclusion). However, even among those who claim to believe in the inspiration of Scripture, there are those who dispute what happened during the days of the fourth kingdom, as discussed in the following verses.

2:44,45 – In the days of those kings, God will set up a kingdom that will never be destroyed. It will break in pieces and consume all those kingdoms. It will stand forever. The vision was God's way of making known to Nebuchadnezzar the future. The dream was certain and the interpretation sure.

God's kingdom in the days of those kings

The dream of Nebuchadnezzar had ended with a stone that was cut without hands and smote the image on the feet and broke the whole image in pieces so it was blown away. The stone then grew and filled the earth (verses 34,35). Daniel said this referred to a kingdom that God would set up and would not be destroyed. It would break down other kingdoms, but it would stand forever.

Note that Daniel here demonstrates the symbolic use of "mountain" to refer to a kingdom. The mountain established by the Lord (verse 35) refers to a kingdom (verse 44). This is a common symbolism in prophecy.

The passage plainly says that God would set this kingdom up "in the days of those kings." Verses 40-43 show conclusively that the kings referred to here were the fourth kingdom, represented in the image by the legs of iron and the feet of iron mixed with clay. This kingdom was the Roman Empire. It follows that God would set up His kingdom in the time of the Roman Empire, or else the prophecy would fail.

Modern premillennialists generally agree that Jesus came to earth and was born during the Roman Empire with the intent of establishing this kingdom that is here prophesied by Daniel. However, the Jewish people rejected Jesus so He withdrew the offer of the kingdom – that is, He did not set it up as result of His first coming, but will set it up when He returns. But such a view means that Daniel's prophecy failed. Since when does a prophecy of God fail simply because people don't like His plan? Was Jesus really so weak and mistaken that He thought He would set up the kingdom, but He failed because of an unforeseen development?

Daniel said, "The dream is **certain**, and its interpretation is **sure**." To say that Jesus failed to establish the kingdom in the days of the Roman Empire is to say that Daniel was a false prophet, the dream was not certain, and the interpretation was not sure!

So, many premillennialists say that, in order for the prophecy to yet be fulfilled, the Roman Empire must be rebuilt and then Jesus will come again and establish His kingdom. This is absurd! The prophecy says clearly that the kingdom would be built in the days of "***those kings,***" certainly meaning the Roman Empire, the ***fourth*** kingdom.

It is generally agreed and understood, even by premillennialists, that this is what the prophecy meant. Many worldwide powers have come and gone since then. Even if the Roman Empire could be rebuilt, it would not be the *fourth* kingdom but another later kingdom.

The prophecy has been fulfilled in the New Testament kingdom.

The truth is that God did build His kingdom in the Roman Empire as a result of Jesus' first coming. The kingdom that Jesus built is the church, and all Christians in the first century and since that time have been in that kingdom, just as prophesied here. Christ is now King and has been reigning as King on David's throne since the first century.

What the premillennial folks and many other people misunderstand is that the kingdom that Daniel prophesied and that Jesus built is spiritual, not earthly, in nature. Like premillennialists, the Jews of Jesus' day thought that the Christ would come to establish a great political, earthly kingdom, defeating all their enemies with military power. Then the Christ would reign as king from Jerusalem over a great Jewish nation like David and Solomon had done. Jesus gave much effort and teaching trying to get the Jews to understand the spiritual nature of this kingdom instead of expecting a physical, earthly kingdom.

Evidence Showing Jesus' Kingdom Now Exists as a Spiritual Kingdom

Mark 1:14,15 – Jesus came to Galilee, preaching the gospel of the **kingdom** of God, and saying, "The time is ***fulfilled***, and the **kingdom** of God is ***at hand***. Repent, and believe in the gospel."

Mark 9:1 – And He said to them, "Assuredly, I say to you that there are some standing here who will not taste death till they see the **kingdom** of God present with ***power***."

Matthew 16:18,19 – And I also say to you that you are Peter, and on this rock I will build My ***church***, and the gates of Hades shall not prevail against it. And I will give you the keys of the **kingdom** of heaven, and whatever you bind on earth will be bound in heaven, and whatever you loose on earth will be loosed in heaven.

John 18:36 – Jesus answered, "My **kingdom** is ***not of this world***. If My **kingdom** were of this world, My servants would fight, so that I should not be delivered to the Jews; but now ***My kingdom is not from here***."

Acts 1:3-8 – ... being seen by them during forty days and speaking of the things pertaining to the **kingdom** of God. And being assembled together with them, He commanded them not to depart from Jerusalem, but to wait for the Promise of the Father, "which," He said, "you have heard from Me; for John truly baptized with water, but you shall be baptized with the Holy Spirit not many days from now." Therefore, when they had come together, they asked Him, saying, "Lord, will You at this time restore the **kingdom** to Israel?" And He said to them, "It is not for you to know times or seasons which the Father has put in His own authority. But you shall receive **power** when the **Holy Spirit** has come upon you; and you shall be witnesses to Me in Jerusalem, and in all Judea and Samaria, and to the end of the earth."

Acts 2:1-4 – When the Day of Pentecost had fully come, they were all with one accord in one place. And suddenly there came a sound from heaven, as of a rushing mighty wind, and it filled the whole house where they were sitting. Then there appeared to them divided tongues, as of fire, and one sat upon each of them. And they were all filled with the **Holy Spirit** and began to speak with other tongues, as the Spirit gave them utterance.

Acts 2:29-33 – Men and brethren, let me speak freely to you of the patriarch David, ... being a prophet, and knowing that God had sworn with an oath to him that of the fruit of his body, according to the flesh, **He would raise up the Christ to sit on his throne**, he, foreseeing this, spoke concerning the **resurrection** of the Christ, that His soul was not left in Hades, nor did His flesh see corruption. This Jesus God has raised up, of which we are all witnesses. Therefore **being exalted to the right hand of Go**d, and having received from the Father the **promise of the Holy Spirit**, He poured out this which you now see and hear.

[Note: The kingdom would come when the power came (Mark 9:1). The power would come when the Holy Spirit came on the apostles (Acts 1:8). The power came on the day of Pentecost in Acts 2:1-4. Therefore, the kingdom came then, and Jesus is now reigning on the throne of David at the right hand of God as prophesied (Acts 2:29-33).]

1 Corinthians 15:24-26 – Then comes the end, when He delivers the **kingdom** to God the Father, when He puts an end to all rule and all authority and power. For He must **reign** till He has put all enemies under His feet. The last enemy that will be destroyed is death. [Note: Jesus will not begin to reign when He comes again. Rather, He is reigning now and will continue to reign until He comes to raise the dead.]

Colossians 1:13,14 – He has delivered us from the power of darkness and **conveyed us into the kingdom of the Son** of His love, in whom we have redemption through His blood, the forgiveness of sins.

Hebrews 12:28 – Therefore, **since we are receiving a kingdom** which cannot be shaken, let us have grace, by which we may serve God acceptably with reverence and godly fear.

Revelation 1:9 – I, John, both your brother and companion in the tribulation and **kingdom** and patience of Jesus Christ, was on the island that is called Patmos for the word of God and for the testimony of Jesus Christ.

> Psalm 110:1-4 – The LORD said to my Lord, "Sit **at My right hand**, Till I make Your enemies Your footstool." The LORD shall send the rod of Your strength out of Zion. **Rule** in the midst of Your enemies! ... The LORD has sworn and will not relent, "You are a **priest** forever According to the order of Melchizedek."
>
> Zechariah 6:12,13 – Behold, the Man whose name is the Branch! From His place He shall branch out, And He shall build the **temple** of the LORD; Yes, He shall build the temple of the LORD. He shall bear the glory, And shall sit and r**ule on His throne; So He shall be a priest on His throne**, And the counsel of peace shall be between them both.
>
> [Note: The Messiah would rule on His throne when He was a priest on His throne at God's right hand, a priest after the order of Melchezidek, who was both king and priest at the same time. But Jesus is now our High Priest (Hebrews 8:1), therefore He is now reigning as King at God's right hand as prophesied in the Old Testament.]

A Contrast Between the Covenants

O.T.: Physical Shadows		N.T.: Spiritual Realities
Fleshly circumcision	Colossians 2:11; Romans 2:28,29; Galatians 6:15	Circumcision of the heart
Animal sacrifices	Hebrews 8:4-6; 10:1-10	Sacrifice of Jesus
Physical birth	John 3:3-7; 1 Peter 1:22,23; Galatians 3:24-27	Spiritual new birth
Physical temple & Holy Place	Hebrews 8:2; 9:24; Ephesians 2:21,22; 1 Peter 2:5	Spiritual temple and Holy Place
Physical warfare; physical enemies	Ephesians 6:10-18; 2 Corinthians 10:4,5; Romans 1:16	Spiritual warfare; spiritual enemies
Earthly High Priest	Hebrews 8:1-5	Heavenly High Priest
Fleshly Jews or Israelites	Romans 2:28,29; Philippians 3:3; Galatians 6:16	Spiritual Jews or Israelites
Earthly priesthood	1 Peter 2:5,9; Hebrews 13:15; Romans 12:1	Spiritual priests and sacrifices
Earthly nation	1 Peter 2:9,10	Spiritual nation
Earthly kingdom	John 18:36; Hebrews 12:28	Spiritual kingdom

Those who expect an earthly, physical kingdom have misunderstood God's purpose. The kingdom that Jesus came to establish was always intended to be a spiritual kingdom in harmony with the spiritual nature of the gospel, the new covenant. A physical kingdom would be completely out of harmony with the spiritual nature of the New Testament.

But like the first-century Jews, premillennialists say the kingdom must be an **earthly** one. And since Jesus did not set up that kind of kingdom, they say the ten toes of the image represent ten kingdoms that will unite to form a revived Roman Empire. Then Jesus will come again and set up His kingdom. Some see the recent union of European states as the formation of this new empire.

Such a view obviously contradicts all the evidence we have presented that the kingdom was established by Christ in the first century but was a spiritual kingdom. This is what God planned from eternity. In addition, however, note that the whole **image** represents a period of about 600 years. Yet according to the millennial theory, the toes alone took at least another 2000 years to form! Further, the Roman Empire ceased to exist centuries ago, so the toes are detached from the body by millennia! What is there in the dream or image that represents this gap of time?

In fact, Daniel 2 said nothing about **ten kingdoms**. The toes are never said to represent **kingdoms**. In fact, the number **ten** is never even mentioned let alone given any significance. This is all imaginary speculation. The passage does mention the chest and arms, the belly and thighs, and the legs and feet. Shall we argue about what specific things the ten fingers and two thighs represent in contrast to the chest and belly? And what about the two legs and the two feet? The error in this view is made clear from the fact that the passage counts the kingdoms involved and there are exactly **four**, no more (verses 37-40). This was Daniel's explanation, and we should not go beyond the inspired explanation.

Since the fourth empire was the Roman Empire and since Jesus came during that Empire, either the kingdom began as a result of Jesus' first coming or else Daniel is **a false prophet**! Millennial concepts undermine the inspiration of Scripture.

Jesus came to establish His kingdom in the first century during the days of the kings of the Roman Empire. He did what He came to do. He established His spiritual kingdom, which is the church, and all saved people have been added to that kingdom since the first century. Those who still seek an earthly kingdom fail to recognize the greatness of our King and the true nature of His kingdom, and they reject that which God has provided them for their eternal salvation.

The dream did not say exactly how the kingdom of Christ would destroy these other kingdoms. However, all the earthly kingdoms in the vision of Nebuchadnezzar have now crumbled and gone, just like Daniel predicted. There has been that no such world dominating kingdom like these four kingdoms since the time of the Roman Empire. But the kingdom that Jesus Christ established is an eternal kingdom. There is no other kingdom yet to come from God on the earth. Those who seek a future kingdom on earth are seeking it in vain and have failed to appreciate the true kingdom established by the true King.

To learn more about the existence of the kingdom of Christ and its spiritual nature, we urge you to study our free articles related to those subjects and premillennialism on our Bible study web site at www.gospelway.com/instruct. (See the section about Man and His Future.)

Summary of Daniel's Visions of Empires*

Empire / Vision	Statue (ch. 2)	Four Beasts (ch. 7)	Ram & Goat (ch. 8)
Babylon (625-539 BC)	Head of gold (verses 36-38)	Lion with eagle wings (verse 4)	
Medo-Persia (539-331 BC)	Chest & arms of silver (verses 32,39)	Bear raised on side (verse 5)	Ram with 2 horns (verses 2-4)
Greece (331-63 BC)	Bronze middle/thighs (verses 32,39)	Leopard (4 wings, 4 heads) (verse 6)	Male goat (vv 5-8; Antiochus IV – vv 25,26)
Rome (63 BC – AD 476)	Legs of iron; feet of iron & clay (verses 33,40-43)	Terrifying beast with iron teeth (verse 7)	

* Based on a chart from *Archaeology Study Bible*, page 1205

2:46-49 – Nebuchadnezzar fell before Daniel saying that his God is the God of gods and a revealer of secrets. He promoted Daniel to rule over the whole province of Babylon, the chief administrator over all the wise men of Babylon. Daniel then requested for his three friends to be set over the affairs of the province of Babylon. But Daniel sat in the gate of the king.

These verses describe the profound reaction of the king to Daniel's interpretation of his dream. Since Daniel could reveal the dream without being told it, this proved that he was guided by God and his explanation of the interpretation was also correct. It proved that God alone had supernatural power to know what no one else could know, including the wise men of Babylon. This in turn proved that He is the true God, the God over all else who claim to be gods and the Lord over all kings.

Nebuchadnezzar fell prostrate before Daniel and sought to offer incense. He gave Daniel many gifts and promoted him to rule over the whole province of Babylon. He would be the chief administrator over all the wise men of Babylon. Daniel then used his influence to also set Shadrach, Meshach, and Abednego over the affairs of the province of Babylon. But Daniel himself sat in the gate of the king. This is an expression for a place of high authority were people would come to consult him.

(The record appears to indicate that Nebuchadnezzar sought to offer sacrifice to Daniel. The nature and intent of this is not clear. If it was simply a gift, that would be acceptable. However, if the intent was to worship him as a god, then Daniel would have to refuse it as described in other examples – see Acts 10:25,26. However, the speech of Nebuchadnezzar indicates that he recognized God as the source of the revelation. Daniel himself had earlier made clear that the power to reveal the interpretation of the dream was in God, not in himself – verses 28,30.)

Daniel 3

Chapter 3 – Daniel's Friends Refuse to Bow to Nebuchadnezzar's Image.

Daniel's Friends, a Golden Idol, and a Fiery Furnace

Nebuchadnezzar made an image of gold and required all officials to bow to it. Any who refused would be cast into a fiery furnace.

Daniel's friends were accused of refusing to bow before the image, so they were brought before the king.

They refused to bow and so were cast into the furnace.

They survived without harm of any kind.

Nebuchadnezzar decreed that no one should speak against the God of the Hebrews.

3:1,2 – Nebuchadnezzar made a golden image sixty cubits high and six cubits wide. He commanded all the rulers and officials of the provinces to come to the dedication of the image.

Nebuchadnezzar, king of Babylon, set up a golden image to worship.

This image was ninety feet tall (nine stories) and nine feet wide, made of gold. He set this image up in the plain of Dura in the province of Babylon. The fact the image was made of gold does not mean that it was solid gold. An image this large made of solid gold would be incredibly heavy. The language may mean simply that it was overlaid with gold (compare Exodus 30:1,3; Hebrews 9:4).

Nebuchadnezzar would surely have human pride in such a statue. He had a dedication ceremony and required all the officials of his empire to attend. Verse 14 makes clear that bowing before this image was intended by Nebuchadnezzar to be a form of worship to his god.

The technical meaning of the various officials listed seems to me to be of little significance. They were all officials in Nebuchadnezzar's kingdom; but it would be very difficult to learn the exact meanings, and I see nothing to be gained by it. The point is simply that the king required all of these officials to be present and honor his image.

When Daniel had interpreted his dream, Nebuchadnezzar recognized the greatness of the true God. Nevertheless, obviously he was not truly converted and did not honor God as the only true God. To idol worshipers such a concept is simply the way they typically think, yet it seems strange to us if we believe the concept of one true God. Idol worshipers may honor a god for greatness and wisdom, but they believe many gods have wisdom and greatness – some are just greater than others in certain ways or in certain circumstances. The fact that they praise a god does not mean that they intend to praise only that god and no other.

To such people, the God of the Bible is just one among many gods. Though they may be shown and may recognize the greatness of God, this does not mean they recognize just one God. Much teaching is usually required for people to come to the understanding that believing in the God of the Bible requires rejecting all other gods.

This would also explain why the people present, being themselves idol worshipers, could fall down and worship Nebuchadnezzar's image even though it may not have been an image of their own favorite god. Since people from all nations across the Empire were present, they would no doubt have gods that they worshiped in their own nation. But they would have no objection to worshiping Nebuchadnezzar's image since to them that was just another god.

Idolatry versus the Biblical concept of God

Idol worshipers and those who practice various forms of polytheism typically use images of various kinds to honor their gods. They believe that the more impressive and valuable the image is, the more the god will appreciate their devotion and will reward them by the use of his power.

The Biblical concept – which obviously conforms to reality – is that no image made by the hands of man can possibly serve as a true God in any sense of the word. The true God is the Creator of the universe, and obviously nothing that men make with their hands could in turn have made the universe, including the people.

Furthermore, it is clear that no image is alive, though people may think that there is some living being or power behind the idol. But the truth is that there is no power at all in the image and no real power in whatever force exists behind the image. If the power that is worshiped by the image is Satan or one of his servants, then there is some power but it is always inferior to that of the true God.

The Bible is filled with numerous warnings against the dangers of idolatry. God repeatedly warned the people of Israel to avoid all the idolatrous practices of the nations that surrounded them, yet they repeatedly fell into the practice.

The seduction of idolatry

Idolatry is attractive to many people because there are many different gods, so a person one may choose whichever god he prefers. And since the gods were invented by men anyway, the gods are believed to tolerate and even encourage whatever practices the men seek to pursue. So, each person finds a god that permits whatever he wants to do, and that is the god that he worships. This may be done subconsciously, but it is a fact nevertheless.

In particular, many idols were worshiped with sumptuous banquets and reveling including drunkenness and fornication. Such pleasures seduce many people to participate. In addition, people enjoy seeing a beautiful image and other evidences of wealth and beauty. They take pride that their image is more impressive than other people's images. They do not like the concept of worshiping a god who cannot be seen. They want to be able to point with pride to visible evidence of their god.

Such thinking has infected even those who profess to worship the true God today. The images they use in their worship and display in their buildings are supposedly made to honor various beings mentioned in Scripture or history. They disregard Bible commands that forbid using such images in worship. They claim that they are honoring the beings that the statues represent, rather than the statues themselves. But this is still forbidden in Scripture, and in most cases the beings that the statues represent are human beings or animals that should not be worshiped anyway.

Here are few of the many passages of Scripture that warn against the dangers of idolatry and worshiping by means of images:

Warnings Against Idolatry

Deuteronomy 4:19 – And take heed, lest you lift your eyes to heaven, and when you see the sun, the moon, and the stars, all the host of heaven, you feel driven to worship them and serve them, which the LORD your God has given to all the peoples under the whole heaven as a heritage.

Deuteronomy 5:7-9 – You shall have no other gods before Me. You shall not make for yourself a carved image – any likeness of anything that is in heaven above, or that is in the earth beneath, or that is in the water under the earth; you shall not bow down to them nor serve them.

Deuteronomy 17:2-5 – If there is found among you, within any of your gates which the LORD your God gives you, a man or a woman who has been wicked in the sight of the LORD your God, in transgressing His covenant, who has gone and served other gods and worshiped them, either the sun or moon or any of the host of heaven, which I have not commanded, and it is told you, and you hear of it, then you shall inquire diligently. And if it is indeed true and certain that such an abomination has been committed in Israel, then you shall bring out to your gates that man or woman who has committed that wicked thing, and shall stone to death that man or woman with stones.

2 Kings 21:1-6 – Manasseh ... did evil in the sight of the LORD, according to the abominations of the nations whom the LORD had cast out before the children of Israel. For he rebuilt the high places which Hezekiah his father had destroyed; he raised up altars for Baal, and made a wooden image, as Ahab king of Israel had done; and he worshiped all the host of heaven and served them. ... And he built altars for all the host of heaven in the two courts of the house of the LORD. Also he made his son pass through the fire, practiced soothsaying, used witchcraft, and consulted spiritists and mediums. He did much evil in the sight of the LORD, to provoke Him to anger.

1 Corinthians 6:9-11 – Do you not know that the unrighteous will not inherit the kingdom of God? Do not be deceived. Neither fornicators, nor idolaters, nor adulterers, nor homosexuals, nor sodomites, nor thieves, nor covetous, nor drunkards, nor revilers, nor extortioners will inherit the kingdom of God. And such were some of you. But you were washed, but you were sanctified, but you were justified in the name of the Lord Jesus and by the Spirit of our God.

1 Corinthians 10:7 – And do not become idolaters as were some of them. As it is written, "The people sat down to eat and drink, and rose up to play."

1 Corinthians 10:14 – Therefore, my beloved, flee from idolatry.

2 Corinthians 6:16,17 – And what agreement has the temple of God with idols? For you are the temple of the living God. As God has said: "I will dwell in them And walk among them. I will be their God, And they shall be My people." Therefore "Come out from among them and be separate, says the Lord. Do not touch what is unclean, And I will receive you."

Galatians 5:19-21 – Now the works of the flesh are evident, which are: adultery, fornication, uncleanness, lewdness, idolatry, sorcery, hatred, contentions, jealousies, outbursts of wrath, selfish ambitions, dissensions, heresies, envy, murders, drunkenness, revelries, and the like; of which I tell you beforehand, just as I also told you in time past, that those who practice such things will not inherit the kingdom of God.

1 John 5:21 – Little children, keep yourselves from idols.

3:3-7 – The officials were commanded to worship the gold image when they heard the sound of music. Anyone who did not worship the image would be thrown into a burning fiery furnace. So all the people worshiped the image.

Worship of the image required

So all the government officials for all the provinces gathered to the dedication of Nebuchadnezzar's image. They were commanded by a herald that, when they heard the sound of various instruments of music, people of all the nations must fall down and worship the gold image that Nebuchadnezzar had set up.

Nebuchadnezzar was the ruler of the greatest empire of his day. People of many nations were subject to his authority. The expression "peoples, nations, and languages" is used several times in the book. The significance is simply that all people who were subject to Nebuchadnezzar were responsible to worship this image.

Anyone who refused to worship the image would be immediately cast into a burning fiery furnace. Nebuchadnezzar had the obvious power to enforce strict obedience, and he commanded that disobedience would mean certain death. Such a command may seem unthinkable in our society, but rulers having such absolute power in those days thought they had the right to give such commands. So naturally, the people obeyed and fell down to worship the golden image when they heard the music.

Obviously, Nebuchadnezzar was making a great display to honor the image that he had made, and that display included the use of many instruments of music. People often seem to think that the more impressive and expensive religious rituals are, the more they will attract people and please their god.

The names of the instruments

Some skeptics claim that some of the instruments mentioned have Greek names, so the book must have been written after the Grecian Empire. But this argument, like most such arguments, is based on the ignorance of the skeptics. How do they know these instruments were unknown in Babylonian times?

The Greek culture existed long before the height of the Greek Empire, and Greek interaction with Babylon and Persia is not only possible but reasonable. The passage says the people of all nations and languages were present at this event.

The *Archaeology Study Bible* says regarding these instruments: "... the Greek words come from the Aeolic or Doric Greek dialects, not the Attic dialect common after Alexander's conquests. This supports a date of writing earlier than Alexander."

This answers the skeptics' argument. But even without such evidence it should be obvious that their argument is merely guesswork. There is nothing here to set aside the evidence for the inspiration and historicity of Daniel as described in our introduction.

The problem of government enforcement of specific religious observances

This illustrates the problems involved when a government attempts to enforce a particular religious observance on its people. Governments certainly are responsible to protect decent and upright people from evil people who would harm them. God has ordained governments for this purpose: to punish the evildoer and reward those who do good. This would include enforcement of proper morality, which is based on belief in the true God and the Bible.

But when a government begins to enforce specific forms of worship and religious observance and penalize those who refuse, conflict is immediately inevitable. The problem becomes a question of which observances will be enforced. When people come to power who do not follow true Biblical teaching, inevitably they will enforce sinful practices such as described here.

It is true that, under the Old Testament, the civil and religious governments were united into one. And the civil government was supposed to enforce, not just moral conduct, but proper religious observances. However, those rules applied only to the nation of Israel.

Under the New Testament the government and the church are separate organizations. This does not mean that the government should become anti-religious and hinder religious observances. On the contrary, they should encourage proper religion. But to require specific kinds of worship and bring severe punishment on those who choose other forms of worship inevitably leads to conflict.

Here are other passages regarding the proper role of government and the relationship of citizens to it: Romans 13:1-7; Matthew 22:17-21; 1 Peter 2:11-15; Titus 3:1; 1 Timothy 2:1,2; Acts 5:29; 22:25-29; 25:10-12.

3:8-12 – Chaldeans accused Shadrach, Meshach, and Abednego of refusing to bow before the gold image according to the king's decree.

The problems created by the king's command would be immediately obvious to Jews. Bowing to such an image was even more obviously wrong than had been the eating of the foods the king had instructed (chapter 1). We don't know where Daniel was at this time, but his three friends were still high in the government. They clearly could not obey the king's command to worship this image.

So, certain Chaldeans came to king Nebuchadnezzar and reminded him of his command that, at the sound of the instruments of music, all the officials in the government had to bow to the image or be thrown into a burning fiery furnace. They then reported that Shadrach, Meshach, and Abednego were refusing to bow down to the image and worship the God that Nebuchadnezzar had set up.

We are not told the motives of these men, but chapter 6 reveals a later incident in which many underlings were jealous of Daniel and used his religious convictions to get him in trouble with the king. It may be that a similar attitude motivated these who complained about Daniel's friends.

3:13-15 – Nebuchadnezzar commanded Shadrach, Meshach, and Abednego to bow before his image or they would be cast into the burning fiery furnace. And he claimed that no God could deliver them from his hands.

Nebuchadnezzar was furious when he heard that Shadrach, Meshach, and Abednego were refusing to obey his command to bow to his image. He commanded them to be brought before him, and he asked if it were true that they refused to serve his gods and worship his golden image. He insisted that, when they heard the music, they must worship his image, and if not they would be immediately cast into the burning fiery furnace. He then challenged any God to deliver them from his hands.

What a presumptuous, audacious statement, especially from a man who had already seen proof of the power of God and had acknowledged the greatness of God when Daniel interpreted his dream. Perhaps he was not convinced that a God who could interpret dreams would be able deliver from the power of a furnace. As the story proceeds, Nebuchadnezzar will learn what God can deliver His people from the king's hands!

Rulers who have such unlimited power in such great empires often become extremely egotistical. They may think they can decree anything they want, and they claim unlimited power to punish in any manner those who refuse their commands. In chapter 4 God will give further demonstration of Nebuchadnezzar's need to humble himself.

This man was the greatest king ruling the greatest empire on earth. His threats were not to be taken lightly. Imagine standing before such a ruler and infuriating him by direct refusal to obey him in the presence of the officials and people from throughout the empire.

3:16-18 – Shadrach, Meshach, and Abednego replied that their God was able to deliver them from the furnace. But even if He did not, the king should know that they still would not serve his gods or worship his image.

Boldly these three young men told the king that they would not worship his image.

Nebuchadnezzar had told them that no God could deliver them from his hand. But Daniel's three friends assured him that the God they worshiped could do so and they said He would do so. But even if He did not choose to do so, they still assured the king that they would not serve his gods or worship his golden image.

Doubtless the experience with the king's foods (chapter 1) gave them courage. But if anything, this was a harder case. The king was immediately commanding them and threatening them with death. In chapter 1, they had been able to reason with the king's servants to find another solution. But this was a clear case in which there was no alternative: they must either disobey the king or disobey God. They chose to disobey the king (Acts 5:29).

Note that they did not know, at the time they faced the choice, whether or not God would deliver them. Nebuchadnezzar's statement had been a slap in God's face: almost a dare to God to prove He could deliver His people. But God does not always choose to deliver His people. Faithful prophets and disciples have often been killed for truth. We can know that God will provide for us, but we do not always know in any specific situation whether He will choose to remove the problem we face or will allow us to suffer and then bless us in the end (compare Esther 4).

Daniel's three friends knew what God's law said, and they knew that to please Him they must obey. They were willing to pay the price, whatever it was, even death. We too must have courage to do what we know God expects regardless of whether or not we know what He will do about our circumstances.

> "Observe that they [the young men] by a special dispensation are ignorant of the future, for if they had foreknown, there would have been nothing wonderful in their doing what they did. For what marvel is it if, when they had a guarantee of safety, they defied all terrors? Then God indeed would have been glorified in that he was able to deliver them from the furnace, but they would not have been wondered at, inasmuch as they would not have cast themselves into dangers. For this reason, he caused them to be ignorant of the future that he might glorify them the more." – Chrysostom (*Ancient Christian Commentary*)

Here we have a clear case that illustrates the principle of Acts 5:29. The Bible teaches us to obey civil rulers and other people with legitimate authority over us according to God's will. But the authority of God is higher than that of any man. When any human being instructs us to do something which, if we did it, would cause us to disobey God, then we must choose to obey God rather than man.

What did Daniel's friends need to enable them to stand firm? They needed to know God's will. They needed faith to trust God to provide the strength and blessings they needed to remain faithful. They needed courage to do right despite the pressures. They needed to fear God more than man. Do we have these qualities?

See Matthew 10:28,29; 5:10-12; 13:21; Mark 10:30; John 15:19,20; 16:1-4,33; Acts 9:16; 14:22; Romans 5:3; 8:17-39; 1 Corinthians 4:9; 10:13; 2 Corinthians 1:4-10; 4:17; 7:4; 2 Timothy 3:12; Hebrews 10:32-36; 1 Peter 2:19-23; 3:14-18; 4:1,15-19; 5:10; Ephesians 6:10-18.

Applications to today

Note that God saved these men, not from the fire, but in the fire. The fact God promises to care for His people does not mean we will avoid all suffering. Each of us today must also pass through the fires of temptation, suffering, and opposition. We may not face a literal furnace, but we will face pressures more or less sooner or later.

We live in a society that is increasingly hostile against God and His word. When we teach people that they need to serve the one God according to the one faith as members of the one body, we too face dangers.

Some Dangers We May Face Today

Social rejection

John 7:7; 15:18-21 – The world hated Jesus because He testified its works were evil. So the world will likewise hate His disciples because we are not of the world.

Matthew 5:10-12 – Men will revile disciples and say evil falsely for Jesus' sake. They will tell lies about us and accuse us of being the ones who are wrong.

Matthew 10:21,34-37 – Family members may be upset to the point of delivering disciples to be killed. Even if our closest loved ones turn against us, we must remain loyal to Jesus.

[Luke 14:26; 6:22,23; Matthew 26:47-50; 10:25; 26:59-68; 27:27-31,39-44; John 16:2; 9:22; 12:42,43; Hebrews 10:32,33; 11:36; 12:2,3; 2 Chron. 36:15,16; Acts 6:13,14; 1 Peter 2:15; 3:16; 4:14]

Personal or material loss

1 Kings 18:4 – One hundred prophets lived in caves on bread and water to escape persecution from Jezebel.

Acts 8:1,4 – Saul persecuted disciples at Jerusalem till they were scattered throughout Judea and Samaria. Yet they went everywhere preaching the word.

> Luke 14:33 – Whoever won't renounce all he has, cannot be Jesus' disciple. Like the three Hebrews, we may or may not suffer this consequence. But we must be willing to do it when circumstances require.
> [Matthew 10:23; 19:29; Hebrews 11:24-26; 10:34; 1 Peter 4:1-4; Romans 13:13,14; 2 Timothy 3:4]
>
> **Physical danger**
>
> Jeremiah 37:15-17 – Jeremiah was thrown into a dungeon for saying Jerusalem would fall to Babylon. When asked again, he gave the ***same message***!
>
> Matthew 14:1-12 – John was imprisoned and beheaded for rebuking Herod for his relationship with Herodias. One of the hardest parts of standing for truth is warning people when they have an adulterous marriage and they must leave it to please God.
>
> Acts 5:40-42; 7:51-60; 12:1,2; 2 Corinthians 11:23-27 – Apostles were beaten and charged not to preach about Jesus. Steven was killed for rebuking the Jews for killing Jesus. Herod killed the apostle James and imprisoned Peter. Paul was persecuted in nearly every city he preached. [Acts 13:14,45,50; 15:5,19,20; 16:19-24; 22:22-30; etc.]
>
> 2 Timothy 3:12 – ***All*** who live godly in Christ Jesus ***shall suffer*** persecution!

What would it take to cause you to fail to stand for the truth of God's word? Shadrach, Meshach, and Abednego were willing to be thrown into a fiery furnace. Are we willing to stand for the truth, even if it leads friends and dear loved ones to tell lies about us, falsely accuse us of sin, and refuse to associate with us?

How much suffering and torture would be required – how many deaths must occur in the church or among your family or loved ones – before you would agree to compromise the truth?

Perhaps the fire that you are passing through is not persecution but temptation or suffering of some other kind. Shadrach, Meshach, and Abednego show that we must be willing to stand for truth no matter what consequences may come. Are we willing to stand like they did?

3:19,20 – Nebuchadnezzar was furious and commanded that the furnace be heated seven times more than usual. He commanded brave soldiers to bind Shadrach, Meshach, and Abednego and throw them into the furnace.

The king was so angry he determined to fulfill his threat and have Shadrach, Meshach, and Abed Nego thrown into the fiery furnace. In fact, he had the furnace heated to seven times its usual temperature. And then he had brave men from his army tie Daniel's friends up and throw them in.

3:21-23 – The men were tied up in their clothing and cast into the furnace. Because the furnace was so hot, the men were killed who threw Shadrach, Meshach, and Abednego into the fire. Then Daniel's friends fell bound into the furnace.

So Daniel's friends were tied up in their clothing (coats, trousers, turbans, and other garments) and cast into the furnace. Because the furnace was heated so much hotter than usual, and because the king's command was so urgent, the men who threw Daniel's friends in were themselves killed by the fire. So Shadrach, Meshach, and Abednego fell down into the midst of the furnace.

The description of all that happened makes absolutely clear to us that there can be no doubt that Daniel's friends would certainly have died if natural law had prevailed. Notice the evidence of the certainty that survival was impossible by natural law or human ability:

* The three men were tied up so that escape would be impossible.
* They were thrown into the fiery furnace.
* The furnace was heated seven times hotter than usual.
* The men who threw them in died from the heat simply from throwing the men into the fire.
* All this was witnessed, not only by the king, but by many other people, since this happened at the dedication of the idol to which all the king's officials had been invited (verse 27).

Once again, I see nothing to be gained by attempting to define the various articles of clothing described here. The exact meanings are difficult to determine, and determining them would add nothing to the point of the story. The purpose is to show that the three men were tied up in such a way that they could not possibly escape. We will see why this was significant as the story proceeds.

3:24-27 – Nebuchadnezzar said three men had been cast into the fire, but he saw four men walking in the fire without hurt, and the fourth was like the Son of God. He called the three men out from the fire, and everyone observed that the fire had not harmed their bodies, singed their hair, affected their garments, or even passed the smell of fire upon them.

When Nebuchadnezzar then looked into the furnace, he asked his counselors if they had not thrown three men into the fire who were tied up. The counselors confirmed that this is what happened. Note the existence of witnesses confirming each aspect of the event.

The king then said he saw, not three, but four men in the furnace, one of whom had the appearance of "the Son of God." This does not say it was Jesus (how could Nebuchadnezzar recognize Jesus?), but he saw one who had such an appearance as he would expect of a Son of God.

Verse 28 says he saw an angel. Furthermore, he saw the men walking around in the furnace no longer bound.

Nebuchadnezzar then called Daniel's friends out from the fire. They had been bound when they were thrown into the fire. How could they have come out if they were still bound? The very fact that the king called them to come out and that they did so demonstrates that he correctly knew they were no longer bound.

When they came out, not only were they unharmed (which would be amazing enough of itself), but they had no indication they had even been in a fire! None of their hair was singed, their garments were not damaged or affected in any way, nor was their even any odor about them to indicate they had been near the fire!

Here we see the nature of true miracles of God. Miracles in the Bible were always events that were impossible by natural law yet they took place because of the supernatural intervention of God. In this case, it is clear that the proof of a miraculous event is overwhelming.

* We have observed the obvious evidence that survival in this fire would be impossible by any natural means.

* There can be no doubt this was a real and extremely dangerous fire – it killed the men that threw in Daniel's friends.

* There was no possibility of fraud – the event happened in the presence of the king and all his officials as witnesses.

* There was no doubt the men were totally and genuinely unharmed – there was no sign of any harm at all and they were clearly observable to all the kings court and officials!

These are characteristics of true miracles.

Some people today claim they can do miracles like in the Bible, but who will attempt this one? In personal discussions, I have heard such people claim many miracles. But always their claims either are not confirmed by the testimony of a plurality of eyewitnesses or else could be explained by natural processes. There is no conclusive evidence that an event impossible by natural law took place. Yet I have never known one to even claim such a thing as is described here, and never have I known one to volunteer to try it!

3:28-30 – Nebuchadnezzar then praised God for delivering these men who had trusted in Him. He decreed that no one should speak against their God because no other God can deliver this way. He then promoted Shadrach, Meshach, and Abednego.

As a result of the miracle that he had observed, Nebuchadnezzar praised the God of Shadrach, Meshach, and Abednego because He had sent His angel ("the Son of God" whom he had seen in the furnace with the men – verse 25) and delivered the men who trusted in Him. They had rejected the king's command and were willing even to give up their lives rather than worship any god other than their own God.

As a result, Nebuchadnezzar praised God and decreed that no one of any people, nation, or language would be permitted to speak against the God that these men worshiped. Anyone who did such a thing would be cut in pieces and their houses made into an ash heap. The reason he gave for this decree was that no other God can deliver in the manner he had observed. He then promoted the three men in Babylon.

Note that, even here, Nebuchadnezzar was not recognizing the God of the Hebrews as the only true God. He recognized Him as able to amazingly and miraculously deliver His servants because they refused to worship any other god. And he forbade anyone to speak against this God. But even so, this did not mean that he himself was ready to refuse to worship any other gods. We will see in the next chapter that still more convincing was needed to lead him to an even fuller appreciation of the true God.

The purpose of true miracles is here demonstrated.

We have already discussed the nature of true miracles, but here we also see why God worked miracles. Always the primary purpose was to give people evidence to recognize Jehovah as the true God and to recognize His true prophets. This would lead people to honor the true God and to obey His teachings revealed through His prophets. This case clearly demonstrated this purpose.

As on this occasion, there have always been false teachers who profess to represent true gods and to have inspired messages that people must heed. Satan has sent such men to confuse people to believe error rather than believing the message given by true teachers of the true God. This creates the problem of how to distinguish the true inspired prophets of God from those who were false. Miracles have always been one of the major evidences that God has given to meet this need. When men who spoke truly for God were able to do events impossible by natural law, then people should believe that they did represent the true God, and they should accept their message as being true.

Passages Demonstrating the Purpose of True Miracles

Mark 16:20 – And they went out and preached everywhere, the Lord working with them and confirming the word through the accompanying signs.

John 5:36 – But I have a greater witness than John's; for the works which the Father has given Me to finish – the very works that I do – bear witness of Me, that the Father has sent Me.

John 20:30,31 – And truly Jesus did many other signs in the presence of His disciples, which are not written in this book; but these are written that you may believe that Jesus is the Christ, the Son of God, and that believing you may have life in His name.

> Acts 2:22 – Men of Israel, hear these words: Jesus of Nazareth, a Man attested by God to you by miracles, wonders, and signs which God did through Him in your midst, as you yourselves also know
>
> Acts 14:3 – Therefore they stayed there a long time, speaking boldly in the Lord, who was bearing witness to the word of His grace, granting signs and wonders to be done by their hands.
>
> 2 Corinthians 12:11,12 – …I ought to have been commended by you; for in nothing was I behind the most eminent apostles, though I am nothing. Truly the signs of an apostle were accomplished among you with all perseverance, in signs and wonders and mighty deeds.
>
> Hebrews 2:3,4 – How shall we escape if we neglect so great a salvation, which at the first began to be spoken by the Lord, and was confirmed to us by those who heard Him, God also bearing witness both with signs and wonders, with various miracles, and gifts of the Holy Spirit, according to His own will?
>
> 1 Kings 18:36-39 – And it came to pass, at the time of the offering of the evening sacrifice, that Elijah the prophet came near and said, "LORD God of Abraham, Isaac, and Israel, let it be known this day that You are God in Israel and I am Your servant, and that I have done all these things at Your word. Hear me, O LORD, hear me, that this people may know that You are the LORD God, and that You have turned their hearts back to You again." Then the fire of the LORD fell and consumed the burnt sacrifice, and the wood and the stones and the dust, and it licked up the water that was in the trench. Now when all the people saw it, they fell on their faces; and they said, "The LORD, He is God! The LORD, He is God!"
>
> Exodus 7:3-5 – And I will harden Pharaoh's heart, and multiply My signs and My wonders in the land of Egypt. But Pharaoh will not heed you, so that I may lay My hand on Egypt and bring My armies and My people, the children of Israel, out of the land of Egypt by great judgments. And the Egyptians shall know that I am the LORD, when I stretch out My hand on Egypt and bring out the children of Israel from among them.
>
> Exodus 14:30,31 – So the LORD saved Israel that day out of the hand of the Egyptians, and Israel saw the Egyptians dead on the seashore. Thus Israel saw the great work which the LORD had done in Egypt; so the people feared the LORD, and believed the LORD and His servant Moses.

The courage of Daniel's friends and God's blessing of protection

Note the great courage of these three friends of Daniel, and the great faith and conviction they demonstrated. We may think we have faith in God, yet how many of us stand for what we know to be right even in cases of far less danger? Don't we often fail to stand up for truth even when we simply don't want to be ridiculed or don't want to lose friends or have people think we are strange?

So we need to learn from this event the importance of doing right regardless of the consequences or the circumstances. Remember that these three men were exiles in a foreign land. They had been taken captive from their homeland because of an act of war but primarily because of the wickedness of their own people.

Now here in a foreign land they were away from their family and their nation. They were isolated from those who would encourage them to do right and were compelled to choose whether or not they would stand alone when all around them did wrong. And on this occasion they were compelled by the greatest king in the world to commit an obviously abominable act. Yet they had the strength to do right and even to plainly state to the king that they would not obey his command. We need similar strength.

We also need to learn that God blessed His people when they did stand for what was right. The story assures us that God cares for us and will bless us when we do right. It is a statement of strong encouragement to us to be faithful and remember that God sees and rewards the faithful. The New Testament nowhere promises that God today will do miracles to protect His people. Nevertheless, He does work through providence for our good. But most importantly, He will ultimately reward us in eternity for faithfulness.

So, let us use events like this as an encouragement to be faithful no matter how difficult the circumstances we face. Let us always remember that God will bless and care for those who serve Him faithfully.

Daniel 4

Chapter 4 – Nebuchadnezzar Learned that God Rules in the Kingdoms of Men.

Nebuchadnezzar Learns the Authority of God

Nebuchadnezzar had a dream that his wise men could not interpret.

He dreamed of a great tree that was chopped down but its stump and roots remained.

He would be given the heart of a beast and graze with the animals till he learned that the Most High rules in the kingdom of men.

Daniel interpreted the dream that all this would happen to Nebuchadnezzar.

The dream came true and Nebuchadnezzar learned that God rules in the kingdoms of men.

4:1-3 – Nebuchadnezzar declared that God's signs and wonders are great and mighty, His kingdom is an everlasting kingdom, and His dominion is from generation to generation.

This account begins as Nebuchadnezzar declared that he had a message for all the peoples, nations, and languages on the earth. Once again this expression reminds us that Nebuchadnezzar ruled an empire consisting of many different nations and peoples. So, his message was for all those who were subject to him.

He began by a greeting them with his desire for peace. Then he said he wanted to tell them about the great signs and wonders that God had worked for him. He said the God's signs and wonders are great and mighty, and His kingdom is everlasting, and His dominion from generation to generation.

This introduced the lesson that Nebuchadnezzar had learned from the events that will be described in this chapter. He learned the exalted and high position of God. Notice that he calls him the Most High God. It is not clear that he recognized God as the **only true** God, but he surely did recognize that God is exalted and has great power. Furthermore, God's kingdom is everlasting and his dominion from generation to generation.

Once again, this contrasts to the pagan concept of many different gods. Idolaters thought that gods did have power above that of men, so they sought to appeal to that power to bless them in their lives. But they did not have a concept that one God ruled over everything everywhere. Rather, they would believe that one god predominated in one area of the earth but another god in another area. One god would have dominion in one aspect of life but another god in another aspect, etc.

Nebuchadnezzar, at the very least, was beginning to learn that God was not just a God for a temporary time or a limited locality. He is a God who rules everywhere for all time.

Nebuchadnezzar had achieved dominion over the people of the nation of Judah. The natural conclusion that an idol worshiper would reach was that the gods of the victorious nation were superior to the gods of the conquered nation. But this was not so. God had used Nebuchadnezzar and his army to conquer Judah and Jerusalem as a means of punishing His people, not because He was unable to defend them. But now He sought to make sure that Nebuchadnezzar did not think he had been victorious over God's people because of Nebuchadnezzar's own greatness or because of the greatness of his gods.

4:4-7 – Nebuchadnezzar had a very troubling dream, so he issued a decree for the wise men of Babylon to explain the interpretation. His magicians and other advisors could not make known the interpretation.

Nebuchadnezzar said that he was resting in his house, apparently enjoying the blessings of his palace. But he had a dream that frightened him, and the thoughts and visions that he had on his bed troubled him. We will see that the reason for this was that the dream obviously had a significant meaning, but he did not know what it was.

So, much like he had done in chapter 2, he called on the wise men of Babylon to interpret the dream for him. Whereas in chapter 2 he did not tell them the dream but expected them to tell him the dream, in this case he explained the dream. But once again as in chapter 2, all of his occult advisors were unable to interpret the dream.

His advisors are described here much as they were in chapter 2. As we noted there, these were various occult practitioners. As such, they were unable to give the information that Nebuchadnezzar sought. They were weak and helpless compared to the superior power of the true God through His true prophets.

4:8,9 – Finally he called for Daniel who was the chief of the magicians, and Nebuchadnezzar knew that the Spirit of the Holy God dwelt in him. So, Nebuchadnezzar expected him to be able to interpret the dream.

And again as in chapter 2, eventually Daniel was called before the king to interpret the dream. We are told that Daniel had been named Belteshazzar according to the name of Nebuchadnezzar's god. And at this time Daniel was recognized as the chief of the magicians because he possessed the Spirit of God. Although Daniel is called the chief of the magicians, the account does not explain why he was the last one to be called. Perhaps it had been so long since the events in chapter 2 that Nebuchadnezzar simply did not at first remember about Daniel's special power.

So Nebuchadnezzar told the dream to Daniel and asked him to explain the dream and its interpretation.

4:10-12 – In his vision Nebuchadnezzar saw a tall tree that grew strong reaching to the heavens and could be seen to the ends of the earth. It produced lovely leaves and abundant fruit so it was food for all. Beasts found shade under it, the birds from its branches, and all flesh was fed from it.

In the vision that Nebuchadnezzar saw while he was on his bed, he beheld a tree in the midst of the earth. This tree was of great height and grew and became strong till its height reached to the heavens, and it could be seen to all the ends of the earth. It produced lovely leaves and abundant fruit so that it could provide food for all. Beasts of the field found shade under it, birds of the heavens dwelt in its branches, and all flesh was fed from it.

Obviously, the tree was symbolic. No tree could literally be so tall it could be seen from such distances and could provide such food for so many people and animals. It was surely intended to have symbolic meaning, which we will see Daniel eventually explained.

4:13,14 – Then Nebuchadnezzar saw a watcher, a holy one, coming down from heaven and declaring that the tree should be chopped down, its branches cut off, its leaves stripped, and its fruit scattered. The beasts should leave from under it and the birds from its branches.

As Nebuchadnezzar continued to observe the vision on his bed, he saw a watcher, a holy one coming down from heaven. This holy one cried aloud saying that the tree should be chopped down, its branches cut off, its leaves stripped, and its fruit scattered. Then it declared that the beasts should get out from under the tree, and the birds should flee from the branches.

The watcher appears to refer to an angel, an angelic being that came from heaven. It had apparently been observing the tree, then it made an official decree. The fact it was a holy one who came from heaven would indicate that this decree came from God (see verse 17).

The result of the decree was to destroy all aspects of the greatness of the tree. The tree itself would be cut down. The branches and leaves, that the birds had inhabited, would be stripped off so that the birds must leave. The fruit would be scattered, implying that the tree would no longer provide food. And the beasts would leave from under it. All this would indicate a complete end to all the advantages that the tree possessed and had provided to others.

> 4:15,16 – *Yet the stump and the roots of the tree should remain, bound with a band of iron and brass, in the tender grass of the field. It would be wet with the dew of heaven and he would graze with the beasts on the grass. His heart would be changed from that of a man to that of an animal till seven times passed over him.*

So whereas the tree itself would be cut down, as previously described, nevertheless the stump and the roots would remain in the earth. They would be bound with a band of iron and bronze in the tender grass of the field. This would symbolize that the destruction of the tree was not permanent. That is, enough would remain that there would be the potential for it to sprout again.

But then the vision changes significantly. What had started out to be a tree ends up being a man! The stump is wet with the dew of heaven but he grazes with the beasts on the grass. His heart is changed from that of a man to the heart of an animal until seven times pass over him.

Now of course, such a thing makes no sense in real life. But we remember this is a vision and symbolic. Strange things happen in dreams, but the important thing to remember is that this symbolizes something. Now it becomes clear that the tree that was cut down is a symbol of a man. He would be removed from great glory and would graze with the beasts of the field. He would be given the heart of an animal instead of the heart of a man.

The heart of an animal does not have the intelligence of the heart of a man. An animal does not live by the standards and preferences of humans. In this case, the result would be that Nebuchadnezzar would live like an animal, eating grass, staying out all night in the dew, etc. But primarily he would lose his sense of judgment and wisdom which he would need to serve as a ruler. He apparently would no longer care for the things that had impressed him in the past as being important.

The reference to seven times is repeated as the account proceeds, but at no point are we told the specific meaning. The times are not defined as months or years or some other time period. Apparently, it is not necessary for us to know. Hailey has suggested that the number seven often refers to completeness or perfection. So he believes that the expression does not refer to a specific period of time but to the fulfillment of the purpose which God intended. When God's purpose was accomplished and Nebuchadnezzar came to the proper understanding that God wanted him to learn, then the period would be complete.

Likewise, the band of iron and bronze that would bind the stump is also not defined here or elsewhere. The significance is not clear. What was bound was the stump of the tree: the means by which the tree could once again come to life and be restored. Perhaps the idea has something to do with the fact that the stump would remain in place and not be removed until such time as it was needed again.

4:17,18 – This was decreed by the watchers, a sentence given by the holy ones, that the living might know that the Most High rules in the kingdom of men, giving it to whomever He wills, and even setting over it the lowest of men. Nebuchadnezzar then called upon Daniel to interpret the dream.

The vision ended as the watcher, in making his decree, declared that the decision came by the decree of the watchers, and the sentence by the word of the holy ones. Again, this would imply that the message was from heaven and thereby was revealed from God. The language does not necessarily mean that the watchers originated the decree but that they delivered it.

The purpose of the vision was that those who live may know that God rules in the kingdom of men. He gives it to whomever He will, and can set up over it even those who are the lowest of men. We will see Daniel's further interpretation later.

So, Nebuchadnezzar had revealed the dream to Daniel and called upon him to give its interpretation. He said again that none of the other wise men in the kingdom were able to reveal the interpretation, but he was confident that Daniel could explain because he had the Spirit of the Holy God.

4:19-22 – Daniel said that the dream and its interpretation concerned Nebuchadnezzar's enemies. The tree that became great and strong referred to Nebuchadnezzar. He had grown strong and his greatness had reached to heaven and his dominion to the ends of the earth.

Having heard the dream, Daniel became very astonished and troubled in thought. Nebuchadnezzar urged him not to be troubled, but

Daniel said the dream concerned those who hated Nebuchadnezzar, and its interpretation concerned his enemies. This part is never really explained, but may mean simply that the things predicted in the dream regarding Nebuchadnezzar would cause his enemies to rejoice. Other commentators think it means that Daniel would have preferred for the events revealed in the dream to occur to Nebuchadnezzar's enemies rather than to Nebuchadnezzar himself.

Daniel then said that the tree in the vision referred to Nebuchadnezzar himself. The tree became strong with its height reaching to heaven, producing lovely leaves and fruit, providing for the beasts and the birds and food for all, so likewise Nebuchadnezzar had grown strong. His greatness had reached to the heavens and his dominion to the end of the earth.

In other words, like that great tree Nebuchadnezzar had become strong and was known far and wide. He had promoted great accomplishments and provided great blessings to those of his kingdom. His greatness had reached the heavens and the power of his dominion was worldwide.

4:23-25 – Chopping down the tree but leaving its stump, etc., meant that God had decreed for Nebuchadnezzar to be driven from among men but dwell with beasts and eat grass like oxen. He should be wet with the dew of heaven. Seven times would pass over him till he learned that God rules in the kingdom of men and gives it to whomever He chooses.

Daniel then proceeded to discuss the part of the dream in which the watcher from heaven decreed that the tree should be cut down but its stump left, and he would be wet with the dew of heaven and graze with the beasts of the field. He said the interpretation referred to a decree from the Most High God that would come upon the king.

Nebuchadnezzar would be driven from among men and would dwell with the beasts of the field, eating grass like oxen. He would be wet with the dew of heaven, and this would continue for seven times till he realized that God Himself rules in the kingdom of men and gives it to whomever He chooses.

So, the tree referred to Nebuchadnezzar, but so did the part of the vision in which one was driven from among men to live among beasts. Nebuchadnezzar would live among animals in the field eating grass like oxen. He would be wet with the dew of heaven – that is, he would live like an animal exposed all night to the elements including the dew. This would continue for seven times until he came to realize the supreme authority of God. God rules in the kingdom of men, and gives it to whomever He chooses.

> *4:26,27 – Nevertheless, the stump and roots would indicate that the kingdom would be returned to Nebuchadnezzar after he came to know that Heaven rules. So Daniel counseled the king to remove his sins by being righteous and showing mercy to the poor. Perhaps his prosperity might be lengthened.*

But we recall that, although the tree would be cut down, the stump and roots would be allowed to remain. Daniel said this symbolized the fact that the kingdom would not be permanently removed from Nebuchadnezzar. After he came to realize that God rules from heaven in the affairs of men, the kingdom would once again belong to Nebuchadnezzar.

Based on the purpose of the dream, Daniel gave advice to the king. He advised the king to cease his sins and become righteous, cease his iniquities and show mercy to the poor. If he did so, perhaps he could lengthen his time of being blessed by God. We will see, however, that all this was fulfilled as God had predicted in the dream.

Daniel's advice demonstrates that these events would come upon Nebuchadnezzar because of his sins. He had become proud, failing to trust in God. He had involved himself in sin and iniquity, and had not been concerned adequately about the poor. There were reasons why God was bringing these consequences upon him, so if he would conduct himself properly he could avoid or limit those consequences.

> *4:28-30 – The dream was fulfilled after twelve months as Nebuchadnezzar was walking about the royal palace of Babylon. He spoke about the greatness of Babylon that he had built for a royal dwelling by his power and the honor of his majesty.*

Nebuchadnezzar's dream was fulfilled twelve months later. He was walking around in his royal palace in Babylon and bragged about his great accomplishments. He talked about how great Babylon was which he had built for his royal dwelling by his great power and for the honor of his majesty.

Such statements are typical of political leaders as they brag about their accomplishments. But notice that Nebuchadnezzar gave no credit to anyone else, especially not to God. He showed no appreciation for his blessings as gifts from the goodness or generosity of anyone else, especially God. He simply bragged about the evidence of how powerful and honorable he personally was.

We may expect such attitudes among such great leaders. It is difficult for those who achieve great authority and power to humble themselves and realize that their blessings come from outside themselves. The tendency always is to exalt oneself, just like those who are rich tend to trust in their riches. It was obviously because of such egotistical attitudes that God had predicted in the dream that He would humble Nebuchadnezzar.

The greatness of Babylon has been described as follows:

> "The city's size and splendor were unsurpassed in their day and included at least one of the Seven Wonders of the ancient world. Nebuchadnezzar presumably built the famous Hanging Gardens – massive terraced gardens with enormous trees intended to console Nebuchadnezzar's Median wife who missed her wooded, mountainous homeland. Also included on some lists of the Seven Wonders were Babylon's great double walls protecting the city, reportedly wide enough to accommodate chariot races. In addition Nebuchadnezzar built or renovated the city's great ziggurat, streets, canals, the bridge over the Euphrates, extensive gardens and parks, hundreds of temples, and the magnificent Ishtar gate, the major entrance to the city on the north." *Archaeology Study Bible* (page 1201)

4:31,32 – As Nebuchadnezzar spoke, a voice from heaven said that the kingdom had departed from him. He would be driven from men and would dwell with the beasts of the field. He would eat grass like oxen till seven times passed over him until he knew that the Most High rules in the kingdom of men and gives it to whomever He chooses.

At this time the prediction of the dream was fulfilled. Even as Nebuchadnezzar was speaking with his bragging words, a voice from heaven addressed him by name. It said the kingdom had departed from him. He would be driven from men and would dwell among the beasts of the field, eating grass like oxen. This would continue for seven times until he realized that God rules in the kingdom of men and gives it to whomever He chooses.

God responded immediately to Nebuchadnezzar's haughty pride, even as Nebuchadnezzar spoke his words of bragging. As the dream had said, the voice repeated that this great kingdom, of which Nebuchadnezzar was so proud, would be taken from him. Instead of being personally exalted as a great ruler, he would be humbled and live like an animal eating grass in the fields.

This would continue till seven times passed over him until he came to realize that he was not in charge as he thought he was. He was not the supreme ruler, but there was One over him. There was One who ruled over all the kingdoms of men and therefore Nebuchadnezzar should be subject to Him. This great Ruler could raise a man to authority or bring him down anytime that He chose. This included rulers even as great as Nebuchadnezzar thought that he was.

> *4:33 – The punishment came on Nebuchadnezzar that very hour. He was driven from men and ate grass like oxen. His body was wet with the dew of heaven till his hair grew like eagles' feathers and his nails like birds' claws.*

Immediately after the voice spoke, that which had been predicted by the voice and by the dream was fulfilled on Nebuchadnezzar. He was driven from among men and lived like an animal. He ate grass like oxen. He lived in the open, presumably in fields, so that the dew covered him. His hair grew long like eagles' feathers and his nails like the claws of a bird.

All of this, of course, would have been extremely humbling. All the great advantages in which Nebuchadnezzar had exalted and valued were taken from him. He no longer lived in the great palace that he had bragged about, but lived in the open field. He no longer ate food fit for a king prepared for royalty, but he ate grass from the ground.

He no longer was pampered so that he enjoyed royal comforts but lived in the fields covered with dew every night. He no longer wore robes and received royal treatment to make him look impressive and handsome. Instead, his hair grew long and unkempt like the feathers of an eagle and his nails grew like the claws of a bird.

In all this God was proving to Nebuchadnezzar that he could quickly and easily lose all these material blessings about which he had bragged. This proved that Nebuchadnezzar was not the source of the blessings. They had been given to him by someone greater than he was, and it follows that they could be easily taken from him. Therefore, he should not brag as though he accomplished these great blessings, but should give credit to the One who was the source of the gifts.

The same, of course, is also true of us. While we may never receive such great blessings and exaltation that an Emperor might receive, yet God has richly blessed us. Instead of praising God and appreciating what He has done for us, if we begin to over emphasize the material blessings themselves, and especially if we began to brag upon ourselves and not give God credit, we may find that all of these great blessings can be taken from us in a moment. Such thoughts should humble us even as Nebuchadnezzar was humbled.

> *4:34,35 – At the end of the time, Nebuchadnezzar's understanding returned and he praised God who lives forever and His dominion and kingdom are everlasting. All the inhabitants of the earth are as nothing. He does as He wills among the inhabitants of heaven and earth, so that no one can restrain Him or question Him.*

Eventually as time passed Nebuchadnezzar reached the point that he learned the lesson that God had said he must learn. His understanding returned, so he praised God. He recognized God for His everlasting existence and power. God rules from generation to generation.

Compared to God and His greatness, people on earth are as nothing. The power and will of God prevail whether among the army of heaven or the inhabitants of the earth. No one has the power to prevent God from doing what He chooses to do, nor does anyone have a right to question why God does what He does.

These are lessons that all of us must learn. God truly deserves to be praised and honored by all of us for all the reasons given here.

God is truly everlasting. He has existed throughout time immemorial and will exist forever. This is not true of any created being: all plants, animals, and people were created by God. None of the idols made by the hands of men are eternal, nor is anything else that people worship other than the true God. See also Genesis 21:33; Exodus 3:13,14; Deuteronomy 32:40; 33:27; Psalm 90:1-4; 93:2; Isaiah 44:6-8; Habakkuk 1:12; Romans 1:20; 1 Timothy 1:17.

Furthermore, the power and dominion of God are unlimited. He has the power to do whatever He chooses to do in heaven among the inhabitants of heaven: the angels. And he has the power to do whatever He chooses to do among the inhabitants of the earth. None of us has the power to resist what He chooses to do, nor have we the right to criticize His conduct. This is the lesson that Job had to learn. See also Matthew 19:26; Genesis 17:1; Mark 14:36; Job 42:2; 26:14; Revelation 19:6; Jeremiah 32:17,20-22.

These were the lessons that Nebuchadnezzar needed to learn. All of us need to learn to humble ourselves before God. His power rules in our lives. He blesses us or chastises us according to His will. But like Nebuchadnezzar, we must all learn to give Him glory for our blessings rather than honoring or trusting ourselves for what we have or have not achieved.

Furthermore, we must not pursue our own will or desires in any way contrary to that which God has revealed as His will. In all things we must submit to His will and give glory to Him.

4:36,37 – Then Nebuchadnezzar's reason returned, and the glory and splendor of his kingdom returned to him. The nobles and advisors again recognized him, and he was restored to his kingdom. Then Nebuchadnezzar praised and honored the King of heaven who works in truth and justice. He can humble all those who walk in pride.

Lessons for Nebuchadnezzar

At the end of the days, Nebuchadnezzar again spoke (as in verses 1ff) and explained the lesson he had learned. Having learned this lesson, Nebuchadnezzar was returned to power as king. He then praised God and honored Him for His truth and justice. He realized that God is able to bring down even the most exalted of men.

These are the lessons that God had been working repeatedly to teach Nebuchadnezzar. We have seen these concepts referred to several times in chapters 2 and 3. Nebuchadnezzar had taken God's people captive from Judah. He had even, eventually, destroyed the temple of God in Jerusalem and brought all of its wealth to Babylon. We can tell from his own statements, that Nebuchadnezzar exalted himself for his achievements.

God still needed to teach him that, though he had such great victories over the people of God and even over the place of worship of the true God, yet it was not because of his own greatness or power that this had happened. God was still in charge and had allowed this to happen.

Nebuchadnezzar had defeated the rulers of Judah because God willed for them to be defeated. Nebuchadnezzar had destroyed the temple because God willed for it to be destroyed. Nebuchadnezzar had taken into captivity the people of God because God willed for them to be taken into captivity for their sins. None of this was because Nebuchadnezzar was so great but because God was using him for His purposes.

God allowed Nebuchadnezzar to win these apparent victories, but then God humbled him to teach him who is really in charge. In the next chapter, God will have to teach the same lessons to one of Nebuchadnezzar's successors.

Note the progression in Nebuchadnezzar's view of God as events in the book unfold.

Hailey points out the following:

In Daniel 2:47, after Daniel explained the vision of the image, Nebuchadnezzar recognized God as the God of gods and the Lord of kings because He was able to reveal visions.

In Daniel 3:28,29, after God had delivered Daniel's three friends from the fiery furnace, Nebuchadnezzar decreed that no one should speak against God because no one else could deliver like He had done.

In Daniel 4:34-37, after God humbled Nebuchadnezzar by making him live like a beast, Nebuchadnezzar called God the Most High. He recognized that God has everlasting power and no one can restrain His purposes. He said that God is able to put down those who are proud.

Yet in all this, there is no evidence that Nebuchadnezzar recognized the God of Israel as the ***only*** true God so that he should not worship any other God. Whether or not Nebuchadnezzar ever in his lifetime came to this understanding is not revealed in the account.

Lessons for us

Mainly this is a lesson in humility compared to God. We must never trust our own strength nor should we glory in our accomplishments without giving God credit. He is the real power in the universe and no one prospers if He wills them not to prosper. No one receives blessings except they be given from God. No matter how great any man appears to be, God can bring him down in a moment. So the ultimate glory and honor belongs to Him, not to the people. No one is worthy of honor anywhere near to what God deserves.

Furthermore, God always rules in truth and justice. We may not understand why He chooses to do the things that He does. Often His ways are beyond us so that we are incapable of understanding. But we must never resist His will or pursue our own way contrary to His. We must never criticize His choices nor doubt His wisdom, regardless of whether or not we understand. We must realize that He always does what is fair and right.

Specifically, we must realize that men serve in governing positions only because God has chosen to allow them to do so. This does not mean that He approves of all forms of government or of all that is done by rulers. Nor does He always immediately punish rulers as He did Nebuchadnezzar here.

But God has ordained the existence of government, and He has determined what work government ought to do. He may tolerate people in office who do not do always do His will, just as He tolerates husbands, parents, employers, and other people in authority who do not always do His will. But He rules above all, and He has the power at any time to throw down any ruler, to determine who will rule in any certain office, and to control the destinies of men to accomplish His will in the universe, especially His will for His people.

It is often in the area of government and the conduct of rulers that people tend to question or doubt the justice of God. We may see good people suffer at the hand of rulers, so we wonder why God would allow such hardships. We see wicked people continue in power and sometimes righteous people are not allowed to exercise authority. So we may question God's purposes.

But it has always been so at times throughout history. Surely good people suffered at the hands of wicked Roman and Jewish rulers in the first century, and God often allowed wicked men to rule even in His nation of Israel in the Old Testament. We must remember that God is still in charge, whether or not we understand. He uses even wicked men for His purposes at times. He has the power at any time to raise to places of authority those whom He will and to remove from authority those whom He will. And in the end, truth and goodness will be victorious. Meanwhile, let us not question or doubt God, but let us serve faithfully.

> **Other Passages About the Proper Role of Government**
>
> Romans 13:1-7 – Let every soul be subject to the governing authorities. For there is no authority except from God, and the authorities that exist are appointed by God. Therefore whoever resists the authority resists the ordinance of God, and those who resist will bring judgment on themselves. For rulers are not a terror to good works, but to evil. Do you want to be unafraid of the authority? Do what is good, and you will have praise from the same. For he is God's minister to you for good. But if you do evil, be afraid; for he does not bear the sword in vain; for he is God's minister, an avenger to execute wrath on him who practices evil. Therefore you must be subject, not only because of wrath but also for conscience' sake. For because of this you also pay taxes, for they are God's ministers attending continually to this very thing. Render therefore to all their due: taxes to whom taxes are due, customs to whom customs, fear to whom fear, honor to whom honor.
>
> Matthew 22:17-21 – Tell us, therefore, what do You think? Is it lawful to pay taxes to Caesar, or not? But Jesus perceived their wickedness, and said, "Why do you test Me, you hypocrites? Show Me the tax money." So they brought Him a denarius. And He said to them, "Whose image and inscription is this?" They said to Him, "Caesar's." And He said to them, "Render therefore to Caesar the things that are Caesar's, and to God the things that are God's."
>
> 1 Peter 2:13-15 – Therefore submit yourselves to every ordinance of man for the Lord's sake, whether to the king as supreme, or to governors, as to those who are sent by him for the punishment of evildoers and for the praise of those who do good. For this is the will of God, that by doing good you may put to silence the ignorance of foolish men.
>
> Titus 3:1 – Remind them to be subject to rulers and authorities, to obey, to be ready for every good work.
>
> 1 Timothy 2:1,2 – Therefore I exhort first of all that supplications, prayers, intercessions, and giving of thanks be made for all men, for kings and all who are in authority, that we may lead a quiet and peaceable life in all godliness and reverence.
>
> Acts 5:29 – But Peter and the other apostles answered and said: "We ought to obey God rather than men."

See our addendum at the end of these study notes to consider the issue of whether or not a Christian may vote in civil elections.

Daniel 5

Chapter 5 – Daniel Interpreted the Handwriting on the Wall.

> **Daniel's Prediction of the Fall of Babylon**
> Belshazzar made a feast for his people to worship their idols using vessels taken from the temple in Jerusalem.
> The fingers of the man's hand wrote on the wall but no one could interpret the writing.
> The Queen remembered Daniel who was called to give the interpretation.
> Daniel said that Nebuchadnezzar had learned that God reigns in the kingdoms of men but Belshazzar had exalted himself and used vessels in the temple to worship idols.
> He said the writing meant that God had numbered Belshazzar's kingdom, he was found wanting, and his kingdom would be given to the Medes and Persians.
> That very night Belshazzar was slain and Darius the Mede received the kingdom.

5:1-4 – King Belshazzar made a great feast for a thousand lords. He commanded the vessels taken from the temple in Jerusalem to be used for drinking wine and for praising pagan gods.

The first four chapters of Daniel's account describe events from the lifetime of the Babylonian king Nebuchadnezzar. In this chapter the account moves to the lifetime of a later ruler of Babylon named Belshazzar.

Who was Belshazzar?

Skeptics have criticized the book of Daniel because of the lack of evidence found outside the book for the existence of a ruler named Belshazzar. I never cease to be amazed how some people will accept the accuracy of secular sources, yet they deny the truthfulness of Scripture unless there is something outside the Bible to confirm it! In their view, the Bible is automatically judged to be wrong except where it is confirmed by secular sources. But if a secular source says a thing, Presto! It must be true!

Why is it not just as reasonable to assume that secular sources are wrong unless they are confirmed by the Bible? The accuracy of the Bible has been confirmed again and again, so the obvious conclusion that ought to characterize honest people is to accept what it says as true regardless of whether or not there is outside confirmation.

Daniel's record repeatedly describes Belshazzar as being in a father/son relationship with Nebuchadnezzar, but this simply illustrates the Hebrew use of these words to refer to a person of a later generation who succeeds or serves in the same capacity as had a previous person. Belshazzar was not Nebuchadnezzar's immediate son, and perhaps not his physical offspring at all, but he was serving as king over the empire as had Nebuchadnezzar before him.

Here is the explanation given by the *Archaeology Study Bible* (page 1211):

> "Belshazzar was actually the son of Nabonidus ... Belshazzar was never formally made king, but when Nabonidus absented himself from Babylon for a number of years, he gave command of the army and 'entrusted the kingship' to Belshazzar, his eldest son, who ruled as king in place of his father. As for Belshazzar's relationship to Nebuchadnezzar, Belshazzar may not have been a blood relative to Nebuchadnezzar at all. The author of Daniel may be using 'father' in the sense of 'father' and 'son' as dynastic predecessor and successor. One sees this when the Black Obelisk of Shalmaneser III of Assyria describes the Israelite king Jehu as the 'son of Omri.' Jehu and Omri had no blood relation; Jehu was simply Omri's later successor. In this sense, Nebuchadnezzar was Belshazzar's father as his predecessor on the Babylonian throne. Additionally, father' and 'son' can also be used of ancestor and later descendant, as Jesus was a 'son of David'... Though far from certain, Belshazzar may have been Nebuchadnezzar's descendant ... If Nabonidus married a daughter of Nebuchadnezzar as Neriglissar ..., the second king after Nebuchadnezzar had done, Belshazzar would have been a grandson of Nebuchadnezzar.

Belshazzar's error

Belshazzar had not learned the lesson that God had taught Nebuchadnezzar in chapter 4, so he repeated Nebuchadnezzar's error. He made a great feast for a thousand lords. As they were drinking wine, Belshazzar commanded servants to bring in the gold and silver vessels that had been brought by Nebuchadnezzar from the temple in

Jerusalem. (Note how this account helps us understand the way that heathen people often worshiped their idols using great banquets, often with drunkenness and sexual immorality.)

These vessels had been dedicated to the worship of God. They were not for common use for men to satisfy their own pleasures. But the king ordered them to be used for the people to drink wine. What is worse, as they drank they praised their heathen idols of wood and stone, etc. The vessels had been made and dedicated for the worship of the true God, the God of the Israelites. But instead Belshazzar was using them to praise false idols, which God despised.

Belshazzar's first error was that of self-exaltation, like Nebuchadnezzar had committed. But even worse he was worshiping idols. And to add great insult to great injury, he used the vessels from God's temple for common purposes and even to worship the idols. We learn here not only the danger of pride (as in chapter 4), and the danger of idolatry, but we also learn the folly of using what has been dedicated to God's service in a common way.

People today make a similar error when they misuse the Lord's church (and its possessions and facilities). Jesus established the church and died to purchase to make it His (Matthew 16:18; Acts 20:28). He dedicated it for the purposes of spreading the gospel, worshiping God, and honoring Him. But instead, many people today seek to use the church and its facilities to satisfy the desires of the people for entertainment, recreation, social activities, etc.

The following evidence is important in understanding the story here.

> In 1854, J.E. Taylor "found four clay cuneiform cylinders written by Babylonian king Nabonidus (sixth century BC) ... Toward the end of the inscription, Nabonidus offers a prayer for long life for himself and his son Belshazzar! Daniel 5 records that King Belshazzar saw the handwriting on the wall that spelled his doom, and it was only Daniel who could translate the inscription.
>
> "Prior to this discovery, critics thought the Bible was in error when referring to Belshazzar as 'king' (Daniel 5:1), since no extrabiblical sources recorded him on the Babylonian kings list. Now we understand that Belshazzar was Nabonidus's son; he was left in Babylon as a co-regent king since his father was away a great deal of the time. This also explains why Daniel could rise no higher than 'third ruler' in the kingdom (Daniel 5:29) – Nabonidus and Belshazzar were king and co-regent respectively."

– Holden, Joseph H. and Norman Geisler, *The Popular Handbook of Archaeology and the Bible*; Harvest House Publishers, Eugene, Oregon, 2013 (Page 82)

5:5,6 – At that time the fingers of a man's hand appeared and wrote on the plaster of the wall of the palace opposite the lampstand. When Belshazzar saw the hand, his countenance changed, his thoughts were troubled, his hip joints were loosed, and his knees knocked against each other.

In response to Belshazzar's presumptuousness, God sent a man's hand – just the fingers of a man's hand were visible, without a body. The hand wrote a message on the wall of the palace opposite the lampstand. The king saw the part of the hand as it wrote on the wall.

The king was totally frightened and troubled by this. His countenance changed – presumably showing fear as often shows on a person's face. His thoughts were troubled. His joints were loosened, and his knees knocked. We would say, he "came unglued."

What a great, expressive way the author had to describe Belshazzar's fear!

5:7-9 – The king called in his occult wise men and promised that whoever read and interpreted the writing would be clothed with purple, have a chain of gold around his neck, and be the third ruler in the kingdom. But no wise man could read or interpret the writing.

Belshazzar called in the astrologers, soothsayers, and other occult wise men as Nebuchadnezzar had done in previous instances. He urged them to read the writing and interpret it so that he would have the meaning of what was written.

Despite the fact that, on at least two occasions, Nebuchadnezzar had found Daniel capable of interpreting revelations in ways that the occult wise men could not, the kings continued to trust their occult advisors. Belshazzar, in particular, had apparently forgotten Daniel and he certainly had not learned his need to respect the true God.

He promised great glory and honor to the man who interpreted the writing. His promises included special clothing such as only royalty would wear, a golden chain around the neck, and the third place of authority in the kingdom. Surely such promises would have highly motivated the wise men. But even so they could not even read what was written, let alone tell what it meant. This greatly astonished Belshazzar and his lords, so that he continued to be troubled and his countenance changed (his worry was clear from his facial expression).

Scholars have wondered why Belshazzar offered only the third place in the kingdom, rather than the second place in the kingdom. The Bible does not explain. However, historians have discovered that Belshazzar himself at this time actually ruled in place of his own father Nabonidus, who was still alive but had "retired" and left the responsibilities of rulership to his son. So Belshazzar occupied only the second place in the kingdom. As long as his father lived, only the third place could be offered to anyone else.

Once again we are reminded that the Bible is accurate historically. How could any writer have known such details as this if he had written this account hundreds of years after the time of the Babylonian empire as many skeptics claim?

> *5:10-12 – The queen said there was a man in the kingdom who had the Spirit of God. Nebuchadnezzar had made him chief of the wise men. He had understanding to interpret dreams and riddles, so if he was called he would give the interpretation.*

The queen, however, came to the banquet hall. (Verse 3 had said that Belshazzar's wives were at the banquet, so perhaps the queen was the Queen Mother: the wife perhaps of Nabonidus.)

The queen remembered Daniel, who had been made chief of the magicians by Nebuchadnezzar because of his ability to interpret dreams and understand riddles. She said he had the Spirit of the Holy God. She urged Belshazzar not to be troubled in thought but to call Daniel, who was also named Belteshazzar, and let him give the interpretation.

> *5:13-16 – When Daniel came, the king said he had heard that Daniel had the Spirit of God with wisdom and understanding. He said the wise men could not read or interpret the writing, but he had heard that Daniel could give interpretations and explain enigmas. He offered Daniel the same reward he had offered the other wise men.*

So the king called Daniel and asked if he was the Daniel who had come among the captives that Nebuchadnezzar had brought from Judah. He said he had heard that Daniel had the Spirit of God so that he possessed light and understanding and excellent wisdom.

He told Daniel what had happened and how the other wise men could not read or interpret the writing. He said he had heard that Daniel could give interpretations and explain enigmas. So he offered Daniel that, if he could read the writing and interpret it, he would be clothed with purple and have a chain of gold around his neck and be the third ruler in the kingdom, just as he promised to the other wise men.

5:17-19 – Daniel said he did not want the king's gifts, but he would read and interpret the writing. He reminded Belshazzar that God had given the kingdom to Nebuchadnezzar so that all peoples, nations, and languages feared him. He punished or exalted whomever he wished.

Daniel said he did not want the king's honors, so the king could keep his rewards or give them to others. Nevertheless, Daniel was willing to read and interpret the writing. Daniel did not want the king to think that he was motivated simply by the rewards. He was concerned about the message that God wanted revealed.

This should also be the attitude of all of God's teachers and preachers in the church today. It is not wrong for preachers to be supported; on the contrary, God has specifically authorized it (1 Corinthians 9:4-14; 2 Corinthians 11:7-9; Philippians 4:14-18; 1 Timothy 5:18; Luke 10:7). But preachers should make sure that they are never teaching primarily for material gain, nor should they determine what they teach on the basis of what they think will please people and lead to rewards.

Before interpreting the dream, however, Daniel had a message from God for the king. He used the opportunity presented by the miracle to make sure that the king understood the lesson that God intended.

He began by talking about the great power that God had given to Nebuchadnezzar. He said that God gave him a kingdom and majesty, glory and honor. As a result, people of all nations, peoples, and languages served and feared him. He had the power to execute whomever he chose and the power to exalt to higher position those whom he willed.

Of course, Belshazzar knew about the power of Nebuchadnezzar. The point Daniel was emphasizing was that these blessings came from the hand of God. Nebuchadnezzar had great power, but it was not because he himself had achieved this on his own. There was a higher power who was over all kings and had given the power to Nebuchadnezzar.

This was the lesson that God had gone to great lengths to teach Nebuchadnezzar, especially in chapter 4. Now this was the lesson that Belshazzar himself needed to learn.

5:20-22 – But when Nebuchadnezzar became proud, God had driven him from among men and made him live like a beast till he realized that the Most High God rules in the kingdom of men. But Belshazzar had not humbled himself but lifted himself up against God and even used the vessels from God's temple to worship false idols.

Daniel reminded Belshazzar of what had happened to Nebuchadnezzar, as recorded in chapter 4. He had become proud because of his great power. God put him out of office, as already described, and made him live like a wild beast till he learned that God Himself is the real Ruler and even kings must respect Him.

But Daniel said Belshazzar had not learned this lesson, even though he knew about it. Instead, he had exalted himself against God by taking the vessels from His temple and used them for their pleasure. They had praised gods who have no power at all, but had failed to glorify the God who gave them life and all their blessings and holds the power of their lives in His hands.

Once again, as in chapter 4 with Nebuchadnezzar, the account emphasizes the superior power of God over all kings, and emphasizes the need for rulers to humble themselves before God. They should realize that God is the true Ruler whom they must serve. They are not in power to achieve their own ends or because of their own superior worthiness. They were put in power by God to accomplish His purposes; and if they fail to honor and glorify Him, He can remove them at any time.

Notice how Daniel describes the false gods that Belshazzar was worshiping. He said they "do not see or hear or know." This is typical of descriptions of idols and false gods by Old Testament prophets. It should be obvious that a statute or an image cannot see or hear or know anything at all. Some who worship idols, however, believe that there is a spirit power of some kind behind the image which they worship by means of images. Nevertheless, the Biblical view is that such is not true. There is no real power at all in the images. It is all mere superstition.

In contrast to the false gods, Daniel described the true God as the God who holds our breath in His hand and owns all our ways. So whereas idols have no power, not even so much as to know what is happening around them, the true God controls everything in the universe. Our very lives are in His hand. He knows all that we do, provides all of our blessings, and can do as He wills in our lives. It is folly to serve as God anyone or anything else.

5:24-28 – *The words that had been written were MENE, MENE, TEKEL, UPHARSIN. Interpreted they meant: Mene – God has numbered your kingdom and finished it. Tekel – You are weighed in the balance and found wanting. Peres – Your kingdom has been divided and given to the Medes and Persians.*

Daniel then proceeded to interpret the writing. The four words written were: MENE, MENE, TEKEL, UPHARSIN. Literally translated they meant: numbered, numbered, weighed, divisions (the passage does not directly state what language this was). The message for Belshazzar was as follows:

Mene (numbered): God had numbered the days of Belshazzar's kingdom and determined to end it. God had decreed that the kingdom would not stand.

Tekel (weighed): God had weighed Belshazzar in the balance of His just judgment and had found him wanting or lacking. He did not measure up to God's standard of a man whom He would allow to remain in power.

Peres (divisions – Peres and Upharsin are different forms of the same word): The kingdom would end by means of a division, so it would be conquered by the Medes and Persians.

The connection between the message God had written on the wall and the admonition that Daniel had already given to Belshazzar should be obvious. Because Belshazzar had not humbled himself before God but had defiled the sacred vessels from God's temple and used them to praise and honor false gods, God had determined that he was no longer fit to serve as king.

God had weighed him like weighing an item on a balance beam, and found that he did not measure up to God's standard. Furthermore, his kingdom would no longer stand. Its days were numbered, so it would fall and be divided between the Medes and Persians.

It is interesting to contrast this message to those that were given to Nebuchadnezzar. Nebuchadnezzar had been admonished and rebuked by God, yet God had never said that he would take the kingdom from Nebuchadnezzar. Daniel's interpretations and messages to Nebuchadnezzar seem much more sympathetic than this message to Belshazzar. God had a purpose for Nebuchadnezzar; and despite his errors, Nebuchadnezzar was willing to recognize God in such a way that God continued to use them.

Belshazzar, on the other hand, appears to be a hopeless case. The decrees are final and spoken with an absoluteness that implies God knew there was no hope for him but to remove him and give the kingdom to others. Some people can be worked with despite their faults, hoping they will improve or at least be useful. Other people are hopeless and there is no alternative but to remove them.

5:29-31 – As promised, Belshazzar commanded to clothe Daniel with purple, put a chain of gold around his neck, and proclaim him the third ruler in the kingdom. But that night Belshazzar was slain and Darius the Mede became the ruler at age 62.

The fall of Babylon

As Belshazzar had promised, he gave great honor to Daniel, including clothing him with purple, placing a chain of gold around his neck, and exalting him to the third place in the kingdom.

But this is a strange turn of events. Why would he honor a man for telling him he was corrupt and his kingdom would fall? We are not told specifically what he thought about Daniel's message. Obviously he could not have been pleased with it, but he had made a promise and been deeply moved by the events, so he did as he had promised.

And why would Daniel want the position of the third place in the kingdom, since he had already said the kingdom would fall? Doubtless this was another reason why he had told the king he did not want the honor (verse 17).

That very night the kingdom fell, Belshazzar was killed, and Darius the Mede entered into power.

There is considerable discussion about the fact that Cyrus was the king when this victory occurred, but the Biblical account says Darius became the leader. The Waldrons and other conservative scholars explain that this was not the Persian king Darius who ruled later. Rather, it was a local ruler named Darius who was placed in charge of the territory of Babylon.

But of course liberal skeptics say the Bible is mistaken. But once again, the fact we have no external confirmation does not prove the Bible is wrong. Why not take the honest approach, since the Bible has been so frequently proved right, and accept the Bible as true until such time as external evidence is found?

These events demonstrate the concept, as often demonstrated in Bible examples, that God would use one nation to punish another wicked nation. Then if the nation that had defeated the other nation itself becomes wicked, then God brings catastrophe upon it to bring it down. In this case, God had used Nebuchadnezzar and Babylon to take Judea into captivity for their sins. Then he warned the rulers of Babylon about their wickedness, and when they did not repent God brought them down.

This also demonstrates why good people do not need to worry or be troubled when wicked people appear to succeed. In this case, people in Judah may well have felt that Babylon was so wicked that it had no right to defeat Judah. But God will see to it that all wicked people, if they did not repent, will sooner or later be punished for their sins.

The details of the fall of Babylon are not related in Daniel's account. Nevertheless, secular records describe a very interesting series of events. Cyrus had come to power over the united kingdom of Media and Persia. After conquering many other lands, he determined to attack Babylon.

The city was well fortified but the city wall actually extended over the Euphrates River. Cyrus had his men dig channels where they could divert the water of the river. Then he waited till an opportune time. This came when Belshazzar and the people of the city where having a great banquet. Cyrus had his men divert the river so the waters under the wall receded. He then led his men under the wall by means of the riverbed and captured the city.

Lessons for us

Note the courage Daniel possessed to deliver these messages of rebuke to the greatest kings on earth – some of the most powerful men ever to live on earth. In chapter 4, he interpreted Nebuchadnezzar's dream that he would be driven from men and live as an animal until he learned respect for God's authority. In chapter 5, he interpreted the writing on the wall that predicted the downfall of Belshazzar.

Christians need courage that comes from conviction. What would you or I have done in Daniel's place? If God gave us a message to deliver to rebuke a king who could take our life, would we deliver it? Or would we keep quiet and hope he found out some other way?

What we would do in such a case is demonstrated by what we **are** doing in other matters. Do we have the courage and conviction to live a pure life, or do pressures from employers or associates, teachers and schoolmates lead us to compromise? Do we go to God to learn the truth and then defend it, resisting human doctrines? Or would we rather have peace than truth? Do we pray and worship God regularly, or do the pressures of physical pursuits come first?

Also note once again the superiority of God's revealed truths to Daniel as compared to the "wisdom" of those advisors with their occult wisdom. Babylon was known for its trust in astrologers, magicians, sorcerers, etc. It was men who practiced these occult powers who could not interpret the king's dreams nor the handwriting on the wall. But by God's power, Daniel could do these things. The accuracy of his ability is demonstrated by the fact the prophecies all came true. (See notes on chapter 2.)

Daniel 6

Chapter 6 – Daniel Was Thrown into a Den of Lions

> **Daniel in the Lions' Den**
> Daniel was one of three governors over the land. Others tried to find fault in him but could not.
> They tricked the king into making a decree that anyone who made a petition to anyone except the king would be cast into a den of lions.
> Daniel continued praying to God three times a day, so the conspirators accused him of violating the decree.
> The king was upset but had no choice but to throw Daniel into the lions' den.
> Next today Daniel was removed from the den with no injury whatever.
> The men who had accused Daniel were thrown into the den and immediately devoured by the lions.

6:1-3 – Darius the Mede set one hundred twenty satraps over the kingdom with three governors above them, one of whom was Daniel. Because of Daniel's faithfulness, he became distinguished above the others and the king thought to set him above the whole realm.

As Daniel had excelled and been given high position in Babylon, so he continued to be respected for his wisdom in the kingdom of Persia. He was given high position by Darius. He was one of three presidents who served under Darius and over one hundred satraps throughout the kingdom. But Daniel was so outstanding that Darius was considering putting him as ruler over the whole empire.

What great ability this man must have had to be so respected. Yet through it all he gave credit to God and learned the lesson of humility that he had helped teach other rulers. We are reminded in many ways of Joseph, how he was taken captive into a foreign country, yet he remained faithful to God. He interpreted dreams and showed great wisdom and trustworthiness, so he rose to highest position.

We recall that we began our study of Daniel by discussing his faithfulness as a very young man in chapter 1. At this point in chapter 6, Daniel was at least eighty years old and he was still serving God faithfully. So Daniel serves as a role model for both the young and the old that at every age of life we can and should serve God faithfully despite whatever opposition and hardships we face.

> 6:4,5 – *The governors and satraps tried to find some fault for which they could accuse Daniel, but they could not because there was no fault in him. They decided the only way to accuse him would be through his service to God.*

These men serving under Daniel resented his position. So, what's new? Rulers today do the same kind of thing. People often seek to rise by causing the downfall of those above them, even their death if necessary. Perhaps the fact that Daniel was a Jew was also part of their resentment.

They hoped he would be vulnerable regarding his work as a ruler, but he was so faithful there was no room to find fault there. So they concluded the only area they could use against him was his religion. Presumably this was one area to which he held so firmly that he would not change; yet the king did not share his beliefs and so could be tricked to make a rule that Daniel would not obey.

What about you and me: are we so faithful in fulfilling our responsibilities that no one can legitimately find fault with us? And are we so faithful in serving God that people know what we believe and realize this is an area of our lives that we would never compromise?

> 6:6-9 – *They told the king that all the administrators and advisors had agreed he should make a decree that, for thirty days, no one could make petition of any god or man except him. Violation of the rule would cause one to be cast into a den of lions. And laws of the Medes and Persians could not be changed.*

So, these men came to the king to get him to issue a decree that no one could make any request of anyone – god or man – for thirty days except of the king. And anyone who did so should be thrown into a den of lions.

Notice that they claimed that "all" the rulers had consulted together to suggest this law, but this was a lie. Daniel had no knowledge of it, and would surely have objected. But the king was doubtless pleased by the honor this apparently gave to him. He did not see the consequence regarding Daniel's religious practices, as subsequent events show. He did not share Daniel's beliefs, so he did not think of the consequences. He had been told all the advisors requested the law, so he did not think Daniel objected. In short, he was deceived and tricked.

But the law, once made, could not be changed even by the king, because the laws of the Medes and Persians could not change. So the king signed the decree, not realizing the consequence to Daniel.

It is probable that the decree related in some way to the heathen concept that the king was a representative of the gods. So most idol worshipers would have no problem viewing their requests addressed to the king as being prayers to the gods. But Darius apparently did not understand the consequences to Daniel and the Jews who would be forbidden by the edict to pray to the true God.

6:10,11 – When Daniel heard about the decree, he went home to his upper room with his windows open toward Jerusalem and prayed three times a day as had been his custom since early days. Then his enemies assembled and found him praying and making supplication before God.

The existence of the decree did not in any way change Daniel's practice regarding prayer to his God. He had always prayed to God regularly, so he continued to do so three times a day. The enemies came, as they planned, and found him doing so in violation of the decree they had plotted to institute.

Keil & Delitzsch, if I understand them, do not believe that the language means that Daniel deliberately opened his windows to pray. Rather, he prayed on the side of his house which faced Jerusalem, and the windows there were not covered (as by latticework or some such hindrance) in a way that would prevent people from seeing. Those who would make the effort to do so would be able to see what was happening inside the house. Of course, it is possible that Daniel's enemies knew his prayer habits and so simply came on him at the time when they knew they would find him praying.

Daniel was clearly a man of prayer. Even though Daniel was a servant of God taken by force into a foreign land where he was compelled to live among idol worshipers, yet he continued to pray regularly to the true God. His practice of prayer was so well known even by his enemies that they knew he would not cease the practice even at the threat of his life.

The book of Daniel records several examples of his prayers:

He prayed for wisdom (2:17,18).

He prayed for the sins the people (9:3ff).

He prayed three times every day (6:1-28). Not even the king's command and threat of the lions' den could stop him from praying.

Christians too should pray frequently. Notice that Daniel prayed regularly three times a day (compare Psalm 55:17). Praying at fixed times is pleasing to God, so long as our prayers are sincere and devout. But Daniel also prayed at special times when he saw a special need for prayer to God, as when he prayed for wisdom in Chapter 2. So Daniel's example teaches us the value both of praying regularly to God and of praying to God at special times whenever prayer is needed or appropriate.

Many Passages Teach the Importance of Frequent Prayer
1 Thessalonians 5:17 – Pray without ceasing.
Colossians 4:2 – Continue stedfastly in prayer.
Ephesians 6:18 – With all prayer and supplication, praying at all seasons.
Luke 18:1 – We ought always to pray, and not to faint.

How often do you and I pray? What would it take to get you to stop for thirty days? If your enemies wanted to find fault against you, would it occur to them to use your prayer habits? Do they even know you pray?

6:12-14 – Daniel's enemies reminded the king of the decree which could not be changed. They said Daniel did not regard the king's decree but made his petition three times a day. The king was upset with himself and worked until sundown to deliver Daniel.

As planned, Daniel's enemies went before the king and accused Daniel of violating the decree. The king's own law said that nobody could make petition of anyone except the king for thirty days, but Daniel was clearly violating the law by praying to God every day.

This greatly displeased the king. The passage says he was displeased with himself. That is, he deeply regretted having ever passed the decree. He obviously had not known the effect it would have on Daniel, and he had no intent whatever for Daniel to be destroyed. He saw he had been "had." It was obvious that the other rulers had tricked him into passing a rule that would destroy Daniel.

The king was determined to do what he could to deliver Daniel so that he did not die. But the one thing that he could not do was to actually change the law. He had made the law, and once made even he could not change it.

Among other things this shows the importance of looking before we leap. Not just kings but all of us need to think carefully about the consequences of decisions that we make. We need to make sure we take our time, do our research, and consider alternatives before we make promises or commitments, so we can avoid rash decisions that we might later regret. One would think that a king would know this, especially when he knew even his own law could not be changed. But it is a lesson for all of us to remember and remember well.

6:15-17 – Daniel's enemies reminded the king that the law could not be changed. So he commanded Daniel to be cast into the den of lions, but he first told Daniel that he hoped God would deliver him. A stone was laid over the mouth of the den and sealed by the king and his lords so it could not be changed.

Despite the fact that the king obviously wanted to avoid sending Daniel to the lions' den, Daniel's enemies reminded the king that even he could not change the decree he had made. So, having failed to find any way to deliver Daniel, he finally gave the command for Daniel to be cast into the den of lions.

However, before he put Daniel in the den, he expressed to Daniel his hope that God would surely deliver him. This showed growth in faith on his part. And it let Daniel know that he regretted the fact that he had made the decree. Nevertheless, he had Daniel cast into the lions' den, and had the mouth of the den covered with a stone which in turn was sealed with his own signet ring and that of his lords so that it could not be changed.

6:18-23 – The king spent a sleepless night in fasting. The next morning he went to the den. Daniel said God had sent his angel to shut the lions' mouths because Daniel had done no wrong before God or the king. Daniel was removed from the den and no injury of any kind was found on him.

Daniel's deliverance

The king spent the night in fasting, refusing all entertainment. It was a time for sorrow and making request of God, not a time for pleasure. Early next morning he went in haste to the den of lions. All this shows his deep concern for the matter.

It is interesting that the account is told from the viewpoint of the king, rather than from that of Daniel. One wonders what fears and anxieties Daniel too may have experienced through the long night accompanied by lions. How did the lions act? Did they threaten Daniel or just ignore him? How confident was Daniel? These interesting details are not recorded.

In the morning, the king called to Daniel to see if God had delivered him from the lions. Daniel responded that he was fine. God's angel had prevented the lions from hurting him. The king was glad and had Daniel removed from the den. No hurt whatever was found on him, just as had been the case with Daniel's three friends in the fiery furnace (chapter 3).

The passage gives two reasons why God protected Daniel.

Daniel had shown himself a man of prayer. But the Bible teaches that, for us too, we must meet conditions in order for God to answer prayers. Specifically, we must meet the same conditions Daniel met.

God answers prayers for those who live upright lives before Him.

First, Daniel himself said that God sent the angel to protect him from the lions because he was innocent of wrongdoing, having done nothing wrong against God or the king.

James 5:16 – The supplication of a righteous man avails much.

1 John 3:21,22 – We receive what we ask from God because we keep His commands and do what pleases Him.

Proverbs 28:9; 15:8,29 – If someone turns away from God's law, his prayer is an abomination. But God hears the prayer of the righteous.

Psalm 66:18 – God will not hear me if I regard iniquity in my heart.

Isaiah 1:15-17 – God would not hear the prayers even of His own people because of their sins. They needed to cease doing evil and learn to do well.

Isaiah 59:1,2 – Your sins and iniquities separate you from God so that He will not hear.

God answers prayers for those who believe in Him.

Second, the passage says that no hurt was found on Daniel because he believed in God.

James 1:5-8 – Ask in faith without doubting. One who doubts will receive nothing from God. We must pray believing that God exists, then believe that He has power to answer prayer. (Mark 11:24)

If we wish for God to hear our prayers, then like Daniel we must have faith in God and must live faithful lives.

6:24 – The king then commanded for the men who had accused Daniel to be cast into the den of lions along with their families. The lions overpowered them and broke all their bones in pieces before they ever came to the bottom of the den.

The destruction of Daniel's enemies

The king then gave a new commandment which, according to the laws of the Medes and Persians, also could not be changed. The men who really deserved punishment were those who had plotted against Daniel. These men and all their families were thrown into the same den of lions where Daniel had been. (This might mean, not necessarily that all hundred twenty satraps were slain, but perhaps just the ringleaders who had influenced Darius to make the decree and then had insisted that he enforce it on Daniel.)

Whereas Daniel had suffered no hurt at all, these people were completely devoured by the lions before they ever got to the bottom of the den. This proved the lions were hungry, vicious, and plenty willing to eat people. Daniel had survived only by the power of God.

Why would the king so punish these men? It was obvious that the whole sequence of events was a plot to kill Daniel. The king had been favorable to Daniel all along, and events showed even more why he ought to be favorable toward him.

But those who plotted against Daniel were not only wicked, self-serving men, but specifically had lied to the king and deceived him. Such men do not deserve to be in public service. And the fair and just punishment for them was the fate that they had sought to give the Daniel.

Evidence of the true miracle occurred

Once again, as when God spared Daniel's three friends in chapter 3, we have clear evidence that a true miracle had occurred (note that verse 27 expressly refers to this event as one of God's signs and wonders). Remember that a miracle is an event impossible by natural law. Notice the evidence that what had happened was truly miraculous and could only have happened by the power of God:

Evidence that a Great Miracle Had Occurred

* Daniel was clearly thrown into the lions' den. There can be no mistake about whether or not he was in the den.

* There was no way to escape the den. It had been sealed with a stone over the opening. There was no way that the stone could have been tampered with because it was sealed with the signets of the kings and his lords.

* Nevertheless, Daniel was not harmed by the lions in any way. When he was removed from the den the next morning, it was obvious to the king and to all that no harm had come upon him.

* The lions were clearly hungry, vicious, man eaters. This was made clear by the fact that, after Daniel had been removed, Daniel's enemies were put into the den along with their families and the lions immediately overpowered them and broke all their bones.

The only possible, sensible explanation for the series of events was the one explained in the passage. God had miraculously protected Daniel from the lions. No such event could have occurred by any natural explanation. Therefore, it was a miracle. The following verses then show the purpose of such a miracle was to lead to faith in the true God, as had happened in chapter 3.

> 6:25-28 – *Darius then decreed that people throughout his dominion must fear the God of Daniel as the living God whose kingdom would not be destroyed. He has the power to deliver and to do great wonders and signs as when he delivered Daniel from the lions. So Daniel prospered in the reigns of Darius and Cyrus.*

The king then made yet another decree. This was for all people in his kingdom to recognize and honor the God of Daniel. He rules, delivers, does miracles, and had delivered Daniel from the lions. He is the living God, His kingdom will not be destroyed, and His dominion would endure to the end. All these conclusions were true and followed as a result of the miracle that had occurred. Nevertheless, still Darius fell short of acknowledging this was the one and only true God.

As in the case of Nebuchadnezzar and his experience with throwing Daniel's friends into the fiery furnace, the king had experienced a miracle which demonstrated the power of God. And once again this demonstrated the purpose of miracles. Miracles have always been designed for the primary purpose of giving people evidence to lead them to believe in a message or a truth from God.

Notice also that Darius said people should tremble and fear before God. Yet this was not because God had brought some terrible punishment on wicked people, but because He had brought great deliverance to Daniel and worked a great wonder. We have reason to justifiably tremble and fear before God because of His greatness and the great works He has done, not just because we fear the punishments He can bring upon us.

Daniel prospered thus in Darius' reign and also in the reign of Cyrus. As discussed in our notes on chapter 5, the passage does not say that Cyrus reigned later than Darius. It is entirely possible that Cyrus reigned over the entire empire, but Darius was subject to Cyrus, reigning in the territory of Babylon.

Note the great test of faith Daniel had faced. When he refused the king's delicacies (chap. 1), it may have seemed a small thing to many people. But those who withstand apparently small tests of faith, will have the strength later to handle great tests of faith. Those who fail in small matters, will not stand in great matters. If we neglect to stand in day-to-day affairs, we are surely mistaken if we think we will stand in face of threats of death. When servants of God, from time of youth on, will stand for small things, they have great hope to do great things for God later.

Part 2: Daniel's Prophecies – Chapters 7-12

Daniel 7

Chapter 7 – Vision of the Four Beasts

> **Vision of Four Beasts**
> Daniel saw a vision of four beasts:
> * The first was like a lion with eagles' wings. The wings were plucked off and it was given a man's heart.
> * The second was like a bear raised up on one side with three ribs in its mouth.
> * The third was like a leopard with four wings of a bird and four heads.
> * The fourth was terrible and strong with iron teeth and ten horns. A little one came up so three other horns were plucked out by the roots. It had eyes like a man and spoke pompous words.
> The Ancient of Days was seated, the last beast was destroyed, and dominion was removed from the others.
> One like the Son of Man came with the clouds and was given dominion, glory, and a kingdom so all peoples, nations, and languages should serve Him. His kingdom will not be destroyed.
> The ten horns in the fourth kingdom represented ten kings. Another would come and subdue three of them, speaking pompous words. But the kingdom will be destroyed forever. God's saints will then be given an everlasting kingdom.

The last six chapters of Daniel's record describe various visions that Daniel received. The visions are predictive prophecies of the future. In many ways they are so amazing that skeptics doubt that anyone could have known them ahead of time. Of course, the point is that Daniel was inspired. The very fact that he did know this information before it happened and he revealed it hundreds of years ahead of time, is one of the main proofs of the inspiration of Scripture.

In this first vision recorded in chapter 7, Daniel saw four different beasts each one representing a different kingdom. The effect of the vision is much like the dream of Nebuchadnezzar in chapter 2.

7:1-3 – In the first year of Belshazzar king of Babylon, Daniel had a dream vision which he wrote down. He saw the four winds of heaven stirring up the Great Sea, and four great beasts came up from the sea each different from the others.

Introduction of the vision

Daniel begins here a description of a dream and visions that he received in the first year of Belshazzar king of Babylon (see chapter 5 regarding Belshazzar). The visions and dream came during the night, but he wrote it down to record the main facts. Note other passages where the prophets were said to have written down their revelations: Isaiah 8:1; 30:8; Habakkuk 2:2; Revelation 1:19; 14:13; 21:5.

In the visions the four winds of heaven stirred up the Great Sea so that four great beasts came up from the sea. The four winds refer to the four directions from which winds come. Each of these four beasts differed from each of the others. We will see that each beast represents a great kingdom, just as the parts of the image in Nebuchadnezzar's dream in chapter 2 represented different kingdoms (7:17,23). Furthermore, we will see that they represent the same four kingdoms that Nebuchadnezzar saw.

Based on that information, it is reasonable that the sea represents society or people from which these kingdoms arose; this symbolism is also used elsewhere (Isaiah 17:12; 57:20; Revelation 13:1; 17:15; 20:13; 21:1). In which case the winds refer to various forces of society that stir up or cause change or turmoil in these various kingdoms (Jeremiah 49:32,36; 51:1).

It is important to remember that there were four beasts, each one representing a separate kingdom as the vision proceeds. This means there were exactly four kingdoms, no more and no less. This is the same number as in the vision in Daniel chapter 2, and we will see that the kingdoms are the same four kingdoms.

Furthermore, the description states specifically that these were four great kingdoms. They were not minor states such as often existed in Old Testament times. These were major kingdoms such as we today would call empires. This is also made clear in the vision in chapter 2. As discussed in our notes on chapter 2, this information is important in identifying the kingdoms, which in turn is important in identifying when the kingdom of Christ began.

The specific meaning is explained later in the record, so for now we will describe the details and then discuss the meaning later when it is revealed to Daniel.

Historical significance of the vision

Please note that this vision, like other of Daniel's visions, is placed in a historical context. That is, we are told specifically when Daniel received it. In this case, it was during the first year of the reign of Belshazzar king of Babylon. Of itself, this fact might seem to have little significance. But it actually accomplishes something extremely important: it demonstrates that the record is intended to describe an event that happened at a specific point of history. Furthermore, we are told that Daniel wrote it down himself.

This becomes important because modern unbelieving skeptics deny that these visions could have actually been given to Daniel during the Babylonian Empire or, in the case of later visions, during the Persian Empire. The revelations are so specific and accurate that they confirm the inspiration of the account. So the only way for unbelievers to undermine the evidence is simply to deny that they were written when the accounts say that they were written.

The effect of such views, of course, is to say that the writer simply lied. The fact that the account specifically states that the vision occurred at a specific point in time gives us only two choices. Either we believe that it did happen at that time, or we believe that the author of the record lied about it. If the author lied, then the whole account is trash and should be totally rejected. The compromising halfway approach of skeptics, who claim to be followers of God but who deny the accuracy of the account, is simply an untenable position because it flatly contradicts what the account itself says.

> 7:4 – *The first beast was like a lion but had wings like an eagle. The wings were then plucked off, and it was lifted up to stand on two feet like a man and was given the heart of a man.*

The first beast that Daniel saw coming from the sea was like a lion in appearance but had wings like the wings of an eagle. As Daniel observed, these wings were removed and the beast was then lifted up so it stood on two feet like a man. Furthermore, it was given a heart like the heart of a man.

Animals were elsewhere used to refer to rulers or kingdoms. See Jeremiah 49:19-22; Ezekiel 29:3-5; 32:2; Revelation 13:1.

In particular, lions are symbols of strength and courage. See Ezekiel 19:2,3; Genesis 49:9; 2 Samuel 23:20; Psalm 7:2; 22:21; 57:4; 58:6; 74:4; Isaiah 29:1.2; Jeremiah 4:7; 49:19; Joel 1:6; Isaiah 29:1,2. In particular, the city of Babylon used a lion as a common symbol. The Ishtar gate was decorated by a long series of a lion images.

Eagles are also often used to illustrate ability to move swiftly. See Jeremiah 4:13; 48:40; 49:22; Lamentations 4:19; Habakkuk 1:8. The plucking off of the wings would indicate that the power to travel swiftly, which had previously characterized this kingdom, was removed.

The fact the beast would be caused to stand on his feet like a man and given the heart of a man would indicate that the fierceness of its nature would be transformed. It would cease to have the swiftness of an eagle and the fierceness of a lion and would become more human in nature. Compare Daniel 4:16.

Again, we will be given more information later.

7:5 – The second beast suddenly appeared looking like a bear. It was raised up on one side and had three ribs between the teeth of its mouth. It was told to arise and devour much flesh.

The second beast that Daniel saw appeared suddenly. It looked like a bear. It was higher on one side than on the other, and in its mouth it had three ribs between its teeth. It was given instructions to arise and devour much flesh. A bear may not be as naturally aggressive as a lion, but can be extremely ferocious when aroused.

Other passages regarding bears include the following: 2 Samuel 17:8; Proverbs 17:12; Isaiah 13:17,18; Hosea 13:8.

We will be told more later, but the significance of the ribs between the teeth in the mouth would appear to indicate that this beast viciously consumed living things around it and had already consumed some. This would harmonize with the fact that it was told to devour much flesh. This command would indicate that it acted under a higher authority.

7:6 – As Daniel continued to look, he saw still another beast. This one looked like a leopard but it had four wings like the wings of a bird on its back. It also had four heads and was given dominion.

As the vision continued, Daniel saw still another beast. This third beast looked like a leopard but it had four wings on its back that looked like the wings of a bird. Leopards are also known to be ferocious and are also known for swiftness. Scriptures also refer to them in Jeremiah 5:6; 13:23; Hosea 13:7; Habakkuk 1:8; Isaiah 11:6.

This one's wings indicate the ability to travel and strike quickly. Furthermore, it had four heads and was given power or authority. Again, whatever power it had was granted from a higher source.

It should be obvious as the description continues that the beasts that Daniel sees are symbolic. They surely are not real or literal since there is no such thing as a lion with wings on its back or a leopard with wings on its back. And a lion cannot be made to stand like a man or have the heart of a man. And a leopard cannot have four heads.

So like most prophetic visions, such as those described in other Old Testament prophets and the book of Revelation, these details are symbolic and are not meant to be taken literally.

7:7,8 – *Daniel then saw a fourth beast which was dreadful and terrible and exceedingly strong. It had huge iron teeth by which it was devouring, breaking in pieces, and then trampling the remnants with its feet. It differed from the other beasts and had ten horns. A little horn caused three of the first horns to be plucked up by the roots. This horn had the eyes of a man and a mouth speaking pompous words.*

The fourth beast that Daniel saw was dreadful and terrible, but it was so different from the other beasts that he does not compare it to any animal. It had huge iron teeth by which it would devour and break in pieces, then the remnants of what was left were trodden under its feet.

This beast had ten horns, but then another little horn came up causing three of the previous horns to be plucked up by the roots. This new horn had the eyes of a man and a mouth speaking pompous words.

Horns are a symbol of authority or power. See Daniel 7:20,24; 8:3-9,20-22; Revelation 5:6; 13:1,11; 17:3,12,16; Deuteronomy 33:17; 1 Kings 22:11.

Eyes are a symbol of knowledge and understanding (Ezekiel 1:18; 10:12). So we have here a man who was wise, but his mouth and spoke arrogant, pompous words.

Once again, we will be given the details later.

7:9,10 – *Thrones were then put in place, and the Ancient of Days was seated. His garment was white as snow and His hair like pure wool. His throne was a fiery flame and its wheels a burning fire. A stream of fire issued from before Him. Millions stood before Him. The court was seated and the books were opened.*

Daniel then describes a court scene in which God is the judge. In his vision, Daniel saw thrones put in place and the Ancient of Days sat on His throne. His description is awesome as His clothing and hair are described as pure white. The scene emphasizes fire repeatedly. The throne on which He sat was like a fiery flame with wheels like a burning fire. A stream of fire issued from before Him.

The term "Ancient of Days" is used again in verses 13,22. To my knowledge, this chapter is the only passage that uses this term. Yet the description clearly refers to God, emphasizing God's eternal nature. He is ancient because He has always existed. The eternal nature of God is also emphasized in other passages: Genesis 21:33; Exodus 3:13,14; Deuteronomy 32:40; 33:27; Psalm 90:1-4; 93:2; Isaiah 44:6-8; Habakkuk 1:12; Romans 1:20; 1 Timothy 1:17.

Other prophets have attempted to describe the appearance of God on His throne. The descriptions vary, of course, since they are all to some extent symbolic. No one can really describe in human terms the appearance of the infinite God. But all emphasize the completely awesome, wondrous, and powerful appearance of God. God's purity is emphasized by the whiteness of His appearance. See Ezekiel 1:13-21; 10:2-7; Isaiah 66:15,16; 6:1-3; Revelation 4:2-10; 5:1-7.

God's power is emphasized here especially by the repeated references to fire. He has the power to destroy in consequence of His judgment. So the description here emphasizes a judgment scene. God is on the throne surrounded by millions of servants (Deuteronomy 33:2; Psalm 68:17; Jude 14), while even more millions stand before Him to be judged (compare Matthew 25:31-46). The millions simply refer to huge numbers. The court is convened and the books are opened.

The opening of the books is also a Biblical reference to judgment. The books record the evidence based on the facts of what people have done. God keeps a record of all of this. In some cases the books that are opened also refer to the law of God to which the acts of the people are compared. This is especially reminiscent of the judgment scene in Revelation 20:10-15.

The other thrones around the Ancient of Days are also commonly mentioned. Who is on those thrones we are not told. See Revelation 4:4; 2:26; Matthew 19:28; Luke 22:30.

Similar judgment scenes and other passages described the final judgment of all mankind (see references already cited above) but in this passage we will see that the judgment refers to a more specific case.

A major lesson to learn again from this context is that the ultimate and the real power in the world is the power of God, not the power of nations and earthly rulers. We have observed repeatedly that power and dominion was given to these various nations. Who gave it to them? Daniel 4 answered, in God's message to Nebuchadnezzar, that God is the ultimate power.

Nations may think they rule by their power, so they often do as they please and end up displeasing God. They must learn that ultimately they rule because God permits them to do so. And what is more, God will judge them. They will fall to other nations or suffer other judgments if they fail to accomplish God's purpose for them.

7:11,12 – Daniel then watched because of the pompous words being spoken by the horn. As he watched, the beast was slain, and its body was destroyed and given to the burning flame. The rest of the beasts had their dominion taken away but their lives were prolonged for a season and a time.

The result of this judgment was destruction especially on the last of the four beasts that Daniel had described. This was especially related to the pompous words that had been spoken by the horn that had rooted up other horns (see verse 8). As Daniel watched, the fourth beast was slain and his body was destroyed and given to that burning flame which had issued from the throne of the Ancient of Days (verse 10).

But the first three beasts had their dominion taken away – that is they ceased to rule. Nevertheless, their lives were prolonged for a season and a time. This is contrasted to the fourth beast that appears to have been completely destroyed. The idea appears to be that the kingdoms continued to exist, but they did not rule the world as previously. But the fall of the fourth kingdom ended, not just the existence of its authority, but the existence of world-ruling empires. No one nation has ruled the world since then.

Again we must wait for further explanations before discussing specifics of the fulfillment.

7:13 – As Daniel continued to watch, One like the Son of Man came with the clouds of heaven. He came to the Ancient of Days and was brought near before Him.

Now there appeared in the visions someone new. He appeared like the Son of Man coming on the clouds of heaven. He came into the presence of the Ancient of Days and was brought near before Him. The fact that He came on the clouds of heaven indicates that the authority behind his kingdom was the authority of heaven – Divine authority – in contrast to the earthly kingdoms which came from the sea, indicating earthly power.

This surely refers to Jesus Christ, the Son of God. The fact that He came with the clouds of heaven is again a common expression for God coming with power (Psalm 97:2-4; 104:3; Isaiah 19:1; Matthew 24:30; 26:64; Mark 13:26; 14:62; Revelation 1:7). But He looks like a son of man because he had a human appearance. The NKJV capitalizes the references so as to indicate that the translators believed this was a reference to Christ. Jesus is called the Son of Man in Matthew 8:20; 9:6; 10:23; 11:19; 12:8,32,40; 13:37,41; 16:13,27,28; 17:9,12,22; etc.

Notice that the events here occurred when the Son of Man **came** to God. In the vision that Daniel saw, the one like the Son of Man came to the Ancient of Days. But from the viewpoint of those on earth, He left the earth to go to heaven. This would fit Acts 1:9 when He ascended into heaven. We will see this is significant as the events unfold.

7:14 – This One was given dominion and glory and a kingdom so all peoples, nations, and languages should serve Him. He received an everlasting dominion which shall not pass away. His kingdom will not be destroyed.

This One, who had the appearance of a Son of Man and came into the presence of the Ancient of Days, was given dominion and glory and a kingdom. It was a universal kingdom in the sense that people of all nations, languages, and peoples would serve Him. It is not a national kingdom of just one nation, like Israel. It included people from all kinds of nations and languages. See Revelation 5:6-14 (especially verse 9).

We remember that the Babylonian kingdom and the other kingdoms that are described as following it were kingdoms that also included many peoples, nations, and languages. This emphasizes the idea that these were inclusive empires. A great nation would conquer many other nations. The kingdom being described here would include people from all nations, and languages, etc.

Furthermore, it was an everlasting kingdom. This is emphasized several ways. His dominion is everlasting. It will not pass away. This kingdom will not be destroyed. Now this contrasts to the other kingdoms that are represented by the four beasts or by the parts of the image seen by Nebuchadnezzar in Daniel chapter 2. Each of those kingdoms would come to an end (verse 12). But the kingdom described here would have no end.

See Daniel 2:44; Isaiah 9:7; Luke 1:33; Hebrews 12:28.

We emphasize again that the kingdom was given to the Son of Man when He **came to God**, not when He **left God** to return to **earth**! This will be significant as the story proceeds and understanding the fulfillment of the prophecy.

Consider the following from Foy Wallace, Jr., in *God's Prophetic Word*, pages 203,204:

> "Daniel 7:13-14 visualizes Jesus 'coming with the clouds' (ascending) to God to receive a kingdom. In Lk. 19:11-15 Jesus represented the nobleman *going away* to receive the kingdom and returning after having received it; he went away to receive it, he did receive it, and returned having received it. Verse 15 says: 'When he was returned, having received the kingdom.' When Jesus ascended to heaven, Daniel said that he went 'with the clouds' to the Ancient of days, and 'there was given him a kingdom.' The nobleman (Christ) 'went into a far country' (heaven) 'to receive a kingdom' and after 'having received it,' he will return. So according to both prophecy and parable Jesus received the kingdom when he ascended to heaven. He will not return to receive it – he went to receive it – having received it, he returns for the reckoning with his servants. The reckoning is the judgment. If the kingdom will not be received until the Lord's return, then the judgment is either too early or the kingdom is too late...
>
> "The parable designates the 'kingdom age' as the period between the going away and the return of the nobleman, which is precisely identical with what is admittedly the 'church age." They are the same period of time."

> *7:15-18 – Daniel was grieved and troubled by the visions, so he asked and was told the interpretation. The four great beasts were four kings which arise out of the earth. But the saints of the Most High will receive the kingdom and possess it forever and ever.*

Daniel reacted to the vision, like we no doubt initially do, with trouble and grief because he did not understand the meaning of the vision. So he went to someone who stood by in the vision to ask the meaning. And that one told him the interpretation of what he had seen.

Notice the interesting expression that his spirit was within his body. The spirit of man dwells within the body of man as long as he is alive (James 2:26).

We also have here an example, often seen in revelations given to prophets, especially in such things as visions. The prophet can tell what he sees and can even express it in words, but he does not necessarily understand the meaning of it. Compare this to the vision that Peter had in Acts chapter 10.

This helps us understand the concept of Biblical inspiration. In many cases the inspired man was simply an avenue or a means that God used through whom some event or instruction was revealed. But the prophet may not have understood the meaning of it any more than we do when we read it. Like us, he may need to study the revelation in order to understand the significance and the application.

Notice that the process of explaining a revelation from God is here called "interpretation." Interpretation of Scripture is a proper thing to do provided we give the proper explanation of the true meaning of the text. Many people have the concept that every person has his right to his own interpretation, but by that they mean whatever view a person chooses to hold whether it is the true meaning meant by God or not.

The meaning of the four beasts

Daniel was told that the four beasts represent four kings who arise out of the earth. In the dream of Nebuchadnezzar, recorded in Daniel chapter 2, we learned that the reference to kings actually referred to kingdoms. Nebuchadnezzar saw an image of which the various parts represented four great worldwide kingdoms. We will see the same is true in the reference to kings in Daniel's image here. Notice that verse 23 specifically says the fourth beast represents a kingdom.

The explanation says that the four kings arise out of the earth, but in the vision the beasts arose out of the sea. So the beasts represent kingdoms, but the sea represents the earth – that is the peoples of the earth (see notes on verse 1).

In contrast to these four beasts, however, the saints of God will receive and possess a kingdom that will stand forever and ever. We have discussed this kingdom at some length in chapter 2. And the meaning here is obviously the same.

So we must conclude that the four beasts represent the same four kingdoms as in chapter 2.

Image of Daniel 2	Beasts of Daniel 7	Meaning
Head of gold	Lion	Babylonian Empire
Chest of silver	Bear	Persian Empire
Belly/thighs of bronze	Leopard	Greek Empire
Legs/feet of iron/clay	Different beast	Roman Empire

The Babylonian empire of Nebuchadnezzar is also referred to as a lion in Jeremiah 4:7; 49:19; 50:17, and is referred to as an eagle in Habakkuk 1:8; Ezekiel 17:3,12. This confirms our identity here in Daniel 7 that the lion with the wings of an eagle refers to Babylon. This shows that our conclusion is reasonable regarding the first beast, and if so then the other three beasts would follow in order. This in turn leads to the conclusion that the fourth beast is Rome, so once again we have confirmation that the kingdom of Christ would begin during the Roman Empire.

In short, this chapter confirms all that we discussed in chapter 2 showing that Jesus' kingdom did begin in the first century A.D., and that therefore it now exists. It will not be established when Jesus comes again, but all of God's faithful children are citizens today in that kingdom. It is a spiritual kingdom, the church. It will continue on earth until Jesus comes again, at which time He will deliver it to the Father. See notes on chapter 2.

The similarity to the beast of Revelation 13

In Revelation 13:1,2 John saw a beast come out of the sea which was like a leopard, having feet like the feet of a bear, and a mouth like the mouth of a lion. It had seven heads and ten horns, with ten crowns on the horns. This same beast is mentioned repeatedly in Revelation: 13:14,15; 15:2; 16:13; and especially 17:7-12 (but cf. 11:7).

The beast that John saw is so similar to what we see here in Daniel 7 that it seems almost certain the meaning is the same. In Daniel's visions, the fourth empire is the Roman Empire; and like the beast of Revelation 13, it had great power to take over the whole earth. It had ten horns, it made war against the saints, it spoke against the Most High, and God's kingdom began during its reign.

On its heads it wore a blasphemous name. This too conforms to the beast of Daniel 7:8,25; 11:36; compare Revelation 17:3. It almost surely refers to the fact that the Roman emperors were worshiped as gods and allowed themselves to be addressed as gods.

But why does this beast have similarities to all the beasts of Daniel 7? Perhaps the best answer is that, although it is a separate beast (empire) and Daniel describes it as being different from the others, yet it includes many similarities to them all. It partakes of the nature of each, but is different because it combines so many ingredients from them all.

> 7:19-22 – *Daniel then wanted to understand about the fourth beast which was different from the others with teeth of iron and nails of bronze which broke in pieces and trampled the residue. It had ten horns and another horn came with eyes and a mouth that spoke pompous words, making war and prevailing against the saints. Then the Ancient of Days made a judgment in favor of the saints to possess the kingdom.*

Daniel then asked about the fourth beast. The description is the same as in verses 7-12, except it adds that the horn that overcame three other horns and then spoke pompous words was also making war against the saints and prevailing against them. And further, the Ancient of Days not only declared the defeat of the beast, but also made a judgment in favor of the saints and the time came for the saints to possess the kingdom (compare Luke 12:32).

> 7:23,24 – *Daniel was told that the fourth beast would be a fourth kingdom on earth but different from the others. It would devour the whole earth, trample it and break it in pieces. And the ten horns were ten kings who would arise from this kingdom. Then another would arise after them, different from the first ones, and subdue three kings.*

Daniel then was given additional information. First, he was told that fourth beast was also a kingdom – a fourth kingdom on earth but different from the other kingdoms. It would devour the whole earth, trampling and breaking it in pieces. This would imply victory and subjugation of the world in general.

Notice once again that, as in Daniel chapter 2, the kingdoms are very specifically numbered. The fourth beast represents a fourth kingdom. This must mean the Roman Empire. No other explanation makes sense, and virtually all truly Bible-believing commentators accept this explanation.

In fact, even premillennial commentators generally acknowledge that the fourth beast is the fourth empire which is the Roman Empire. They believe that God intended Jesus to come to earth during the Roman Empire and establish His kingdom. But they claim He could not do so because the Jews unexpectedly rejected Him and killed Him, so God established the church instead of the kingdom that he intended to establish.

So, to scotch up the apparent mistake that God made, the premillennial view often is that the ten horns in the fourth kingdom represent ten kingdoms that will be established at the time of the Jesus' second coming. They will constitute a renewal of the Roman Empire; and in the days of those ten kings, Jesus will establish His earthly kingdom in fulfillment of the prophecy.

But consider the problems involved in this explanation. In the first place, if this is the proper explanation, then the premillennial folks are mistaken when they say Jesus expected to establish His kingdom the first time He came to earth. If the prophecy means that He would actually establish the kingdom centuries later in the days of the ten kings, then it would not be during Jesus' first coming. So which is it? Are they wrong when they say Jesus intended to establish the kingdom the first time He came, or are they wrong in their explanation of Daniel's prophecy?

Furthermore, note that the ten horns are **part of** the fourth beast (verses 8,20). They are ten **kings** arising from the fourth kingdom (verses 23,24). They are not ten **kingdoms** that originate thousands of years later, separate from the fourth kingdom. They are kings that reigned while Rome still existed, not 2000 years after it had been destroyed.

Nevertheless, there are details that are difficult to explain. What is the significance of the ten kings? The vision is highly symbolic, so why should we consider the numbers to be literal? Ten is often the number of completeness in Scripture, so perhaps the number ten simply refers to the complete number of emperors that would rule in the Roman Empire.

What is represented by the three horns that were removed by the one horn? Remembering that the numbers are often symbolic here, Hailey suggests that the one horn simply represents the various Roman emperors that persecuted the church. And the three that fell before them simply represent those whom they removed.

King acknowledges that the number ten can be symbolic, but then he proceeds to name ten Roman emperors who he believes are represented by the ten horns: Augustus, Tiberius, Caligula, Claudius, Nero, Galba, Otho, Vitellius, Vespasian, and Titus. He then concludes that Domitian is the eleventh horn that pushes out three other horns. He then became the source of terrible persecution against God's people. (Those who are interested may see his commentary for his lengthy defense of this view.)

Regardless of what view is the correct explanation, it cannot be denied that the vision teaches that the kingdom of the Messiah would begin during the period of the Roman Empire. This is the important point to remember having primary application to the church is revealed in the New Testament.

> 7:25,26 – *The king will speak pompous words against the Most High. He will persecute the saints and intend to change times and law. The saints were put under his power for a time and times and half a time. But when the court is seated, they will take away his dominion to consume and destroy it forever.*

Here is much more information. This one king who speaks pompous words against the Most High, will persecute the saints and attempt to change the times and the law. The saints will be given into his hand – that is under his control – for a time and times and half a time. But when that Ancient of Days sits on the seat of judgment, his dominion will be removed and destroyed forever.

This also fits well with the prophecy of Revelation 13. There the beast exalted himself against the saints and persecuted them. If we are right in our explanation there, then this would refer to the persecution raised by the Roman Empire against Christians. And the pompous words would refer to the claim of many of the Caesars to be gods who deserved to be worshiped as God. God's people would be persecuted because they refused to worship the Caesars.

They would prevail for a time and times and half a time – that is 3½ times. This would continue until God sat in judgment and took away his dominion to destroy it forever. But what is the meaning here?

If we take the word "time" as used here to refer to a year, then the period of persecution against the saints would last for 3½ years. But 3½ years would equal 42 months, the same time period as described in Revelation 11:2; 13:5. It would also equal 1260 days (with each month equaling 30 days) as described in Revelation 11:3; 12:6. All these passages refer to a period of great persecution described by references to a similar time period. And if our conclusions are correct, then the persecution would be brought upon the Christians by the Roman Empire.

However, since these prophecies are highly symbolic, there is little reason to think the time period is literally 3½ years. Some suggest that, since the number seven represents perfection or completeness in Scripture (based on the perfect creation that God completed in seven days), then half that number may represent a short time which is broken, incomplete, or indefinite. So the persecution continues against the saints; but then it is interrupted, the Roman Empire is destroyed, and the kingdom of God prevails. These ideas seem in general to fit the prophecy here and elsewhere in Scripture.

> 7:27,28 – *Then the kingdom and dominion and greatness of the kingdoms under the whole earth would be given to the saints. This kingdom is an everlasting kingdom and all dominions should serve and obey God. That is the end of Daniel's account. He was greatly troubled but kept the matter in his heart.*

The king of the Roman Empire would fall, but God's kingdom would continue forever. His people would continue serving Him with people of all dominions. Again, if our explanation is correct, the point is, as in chapter 2, that the kingdom established by Christ would continue forever. It is not an earthly kingdom, but a spiritual kingdom. It is the church. It continues even till today, and people of all nations have been granted the privilege to become part of it.

The main lesson for us to learn here is that ultimately God and His people will prevail. God is the greatest power of all, and He assures us that He will win the victory and those who are with him will be victorious. Verse 22 says that God's judgment was made in favor of the saints. Earthly kingdoms come and go, but God's kingdom will prevail and remain. Such has been the course of history.

It is easy for us to be discouraged and troubled because we see the wickedness of nations and rulers, and we wonder when justice will be done. One major lesson of the book of Daniel is that nations will not continue and ultimately prevail if they become wicked and fail to serve God's purpose. In His power and providence God will see to it that wicked nations are destroyed. But the kingdom of the Lord will continue till the end of time.

This is a very challenging vision. Obviously Daniel did not understand it. Like many Old Testament prophecies, many details may not be understood until the fulfillment. But if we are correct that it has been fulfilled, still some details are difficult.

Other details in the prophecy

We have suggested a general explanation of the prophecy in its fulfillment. But here are a number of the details that remain to be explained. Perhaps no explanation is needed, but one wonders why the details are given if they have no meaning.

Regarding the first beast (the lion with wings like an eagle), why were the wings plucked off so it stood like a man and had a man's heart? A possible suggestion is that the wings represented the speed with which the Babylonian Empire under Nebuchadnezzar conquered the nations around them by the power of God. When God's purpose had been accomplished, He withdrew Nebuchadnezzar's ability to continue capturing other lands. At that point, Nebuchadnezzar's power became simply the power of a man without further aid from God. It may also be that, when Babylon's work of conquering ceased, king

Nebuchadnezzar eventually learned to act more like a human and less like a beast.

Why was the bear, the second beast, raised up on its side, and why did it have three ribs in its mouth? The bear represents the Medo Persian Empire. The vision in Daniel 8:3 pictures that empire as a ram with two horns, but one was higher than the other. This may be explained to mean that the empire was an alliance between the Medes and the Persians, but the Persians were more powerful. In the same way, perhaps the fact one side of the bear is higher than the other similarly illustrates the fact that Persia was more powerful than the Medes.

The bones in the mouth of the bear may simply indicate the power of the empire to consume other nations. The number three most likely represents nothing literally but is simply a symbol for other nations that were defeated.

Why did the leopard, the third beast, have wings like a bird and four heads? As with Babylon, the wings may illustrate the quickness with which it came to power. Alexander the great conquered the world in just a very short time. But after he died the kingdom was divided into four kingdoms, which may be represented by the four heads.

Daniel 8

Chapter 8 – Vision of the Ram and the Male Goat

> **Vision of the Ram and the Male Goat**
> Daniel saw a ram with two horns pushing west, south, and north.
> A male goat with a notable horn came from the west and cast down the ram.
> The notable horn was replaced by four horns, one of which grew towards the Glorious Land.
> He exalted himself so the sacrifices and place of sanctuary were cast down.
> After two thousand three hundred days the sanctuary will be cleansed.
> The ram with two horns represents the Medes and Persians.
> The male goat is Greece from which would come four kingdoms.
> One of the kings would attack the holy people but he will be broken.

8:1,2 – Daniel saw another vision, this one in the third year of King Belshazzar. In the vision, he was in Shushan in the province of Elam by the River Ulai.

In this chapter Daniel records the second of the visions that he had seen and the lessons that he learned as a result. This vision occurred in the third year of the reign of king Belshazzar after the first one that he had seen as recorded in chapter 7, which he saw in the first year of Belshazzar.

In this vision, he saw himself in Shushan in the province of Elam beside the River Ulai. Shushan was located east of Babylon. The Ulai River ran next to Shushan (see a **map**). King says that it was a canal located northeast of Shushan, and was mentioned in one of the inscriptions of Ashurbanipal. Apparently Daniel himself was physically still in the region of the Babylonian Empire, yet in the vision he saw himself in the city that was to become a capital city of the Persian

Empire (Nehemiah 1:1; Esther 1:2,5; 2:3,5). This seems to be significant in interpreting the dream.

The dream of Nebuchadnezzar in chapter 2 and the vision of Daniel in chapter 7 had described four successive world kingdoms. These revelations had emphasized the first kingdom and especially the fourth kingdom. The first kingdom had been that of the Babylonians, and the last that of the Romans. The latter was especially important because during that kingdom God would set up His kingdom.

In this vision Daniel receives much more information about the middle two kingdoms: the empire the Medes and Persians and the empire of the Greeks. This would also be important to the people of Israel because of the suffering that is predicted to come upon them in the period of the Greeks.

Notice that Daniel expressly states that this vision appeared to him, that is to Daniel. He names himself as the one to whom the vision appeared. This makes it quite clear that he is the author of this description of the vision. To claim that someone else other than Daniel wrote the book is simply unbelief.

8:3,4 – Standing beside the river Daniel saw a ram with two horns, and the one that came up last was a higher horn. The ram pushed to the west, north, and south, no animal being able to withstand him or deliver from his hand. He did as he chose and became great.

In this vision Daniel also saw animals as he had in the previous vision. However, they were different animals with different characteristics. First, he saw a ram with two horns, the horns being high. But the one that came up last was higher than the other horn. As usual, a horn represents strength and authority (1 Kings 22:11; Zechariah 1:18; Psalm 75:4).

This ram pushed to the west, north, and south. This would certainly fit the Medo Persian Empire. It originated in the far eastern territory of the empire it eventually developed. From there it conquered nations to the west, north, and south, but did not extend itself to the east.

No one was able to withstand him or deliver from his hand. He did as he chose to do and became great The fact that it became great once again implies an empire, not just a local king or state. It surely would not fit any empire of the Medes alone separate from the Persians.

This latter description sounds like the ram once again represents a kingdom. The kingdom conquered other nations around it being so strong that no one could withstand it. We will see the specific description later as we proceed.

Once again we will see that an explanation is given later on to help us understand specifics.

8:5-7 – Then a male goat, having a notable horn between his eyes, came from the west moving across the surface of the earth without touching the ground. He ran at the ram with furious power confronting him. He was moved with rage and attacked the ram and broke his two horns. The ram could not withstand the goat but was cast to the ground and trampled.

Next Daniel saw a male goat that came from the west. The fact this goat came from the west to attack the Medo Persian Empire would fit perfectly with the Grecian Empire of Alexander the Great. It began far to the west and came to attack the Medes and Persians.

It had a notable horn between its eyes, and moved across the surface of the earth without touching the ground. It came to the ram that had the two horns, was moved with rage against him, and attacked him running at him with furious power.

The result was that he broke the two horns of the ram because the ram did not have the power to withstand him. The goat cast the ram to the ground and trampled him, no one being able to deliver the ram from the power of the goat.

Once again, it sounds like the ram and the goat represent powerful kingdoms. The one coming from the west attacked the ram with the two horns, thoroughly defeating it because it did not have the power to withstand him. We will see the explanation given later, but it sounds like these once again represent two of the great kingdoms that we have seen already described in chapter 2 and chapter 7.

8:8,9 – The male goat became very great, but when he was strong the large horn was broken and in its place came up four notable horns toward the winds of heaven. Out of one of these horns came a little horn which grew exceedingly great toward the south and the east and toward the glorious land.

The male goat had been victorious against the ram, and had became very great. But when it was strong, the large horn was broken. In his place came four notable horns toward the winds of heaven. And out of one of these horns came a little horn which grew exceedingly great toward the south and toward the east and toward the glorious land.

In chapter 7 the horns had represented the kings. This description sounds very much like the horns here also refer to kings. The male goat originally had one great king. But that king died and was replaced by four kings in four different directions. And from one of those kings came a small king that became especially great in the area of the south and the east, including God's special land of Israel (Judah).

King lists various passages that describe the land of Israel by terms similar to the "Glorious Land": Ezekiel 20:6,15; Zechariah 7:14; Jeremiah 3:19; Malachi 3:12; Psalm 50:2; Lamentations 2:15.

Once again we will see these details explained later.

8:10-12 – This little horn grew up to the host of heaven and cast some of them and some of the stars to the ground and trampled them. He exalted himself as Prince of the host and caused the daily sacrifice to be taken away and the place of the sanctuary cast down. Because of transgression, the horn had an army to oppose the daily sacrifices, cast the truth down, yet prosper.

The little horn exalted himself.

This little horn, that had grown strong toward the holy land, then grew up to the host of heaven casting some of them down, casting down some stars to the ground and trampling them. He exalted himself as high as the Prince of the host. He caused the daily sacrifices to be taken away and the place of His sanctuary to be cast down. Because of transgression, he received an army by which he opposed the daily sacrifices and cast down the truth to the ground. In all this he nevertheless prospered.

Once again, it sounds like this little horn represents a king. The host of heaven may symbolize God's people as a whole, and the stars symbolize leaders (Hailey compares this to Joel 2:10; 3:15; Isaiah 13:10). If that is correct, then the Prince of the host must be God Himself who rules over the people of God (note that it is His sanctuary). So the idea is that this king abused the people of God, even casting down those who held high positions.

He exalted himself as though he was as high as God. He had the power to cause the daily sacrifices to be taken away and cast down the place of the sanctuary, opposing the truth (God's law). He prospered in all of this because of transgression; God suffered this to happen because of the sins of the people.

Again, further explanation must be given, but this appears to be the description of a king (see verse 25).

(Verse 12 is apparently quite difficult of translation.)

He prospered despite his evil.

Notice that, even though this wicked person cast the truth to the ground, nevertheless he prospered for a while. Wicked people do sometimes prosper. It is easy for us to think that wicked people should never prosper in this life and that justice demands that evil people suffer and good people be rewarded. But the ultimate rewards from God come after this life, not during life.

In many cases recorded in Scripture, evil people succeeded in achieving their goals because God was using them for His purposes.

Many times He allowed them to punish His people because of their sins. In the book of Judges God often allowed nations around Israel to oppress them for the purpose of leading them to repentance. He allowed the Assyrians to take the northern tribes of Israel into captivity and later the Babylonians took Judah into captivity and destroyed Jerusalem and the temple because of the sins of the people.

Often the nation that God used for these purposes was wicked and did not realize that they were being used by God. In many cases they thought they were being successful because they were so powerful, and often they went beyond what God intended for them to do. In such cases God often brought destruction on those people for their pride and disrespect for Him, even after He used them for His purposes.

We need to remember this in our observations of society around us today. Just because people appear to be prosperous in this life does not mean that God approves of them. And just because people suffer in this life does not mean they are in sin.

8:13,14 – Daniel then heard two holy ones speak, and one asked the other how long the vision would be concerning the daily sacrifices and the transgression of desolation, the sanctuary and the host to be trampled under foot. The answer was two thousand three hundred days, then the sanctuary would be cleansed.

In his vision, Daniel had seen the daily sacrifices taken away and the sanctuary cast down. Now further information was given about this in which two holy ones (presumably angels) spoke. One asked the other how long this would be: that is, how long this condition would continue in which the sacrifices would be taken away and the sanctuary and the host trampled underfoot.

The answer that was given was two thousand three hundred days. Then the sanctuary would be cleansed. In Daniel 7:7,11,25 we discussed Daniel's prophecy in which God's people would be persecuted one thousand two hundred sixty days, which amounted to 3½ years or forty-two months. But here a different length of time is given, implying a different event.

(However, King points out that the 2300 days may be taken to refer to 2300 evenings and mornings. Since the context refers to the evening and morning sacrifices, some conclude that the reference is to 2300 evenings and mornings for which sacrifices were offered, which would amount to 1150 twenty-four-hour days. This would be much closer to the time period in these other prophecies.)

This event sounds like it refers to one who would overrun the temple and cause the worship there to cease. However, after a period of desolation, the temple would be cleansed and the sacrifice and service there would be continued. Once again, we will learn more later.

8:15,16 – After he had seen the vision, Daniel sought the meaning. Someone who looked like a man stood before him and a man's voice came from the area of the Ulai River and urged Gabriel to make Daniel understand the vision.

So at this point Daniel was contemplating the vision that he had seen. Of course, he was confused about it much like we would be, and much like we are even now as we first read it without explanation. And once again we see that prophets often received visions or revelations that they did not themselves understand.

But one who looked like a man stood before him and instruction came from the area of the river calling one by the name Gabriel and instructing him to give Daniel an understanding of the vision. It would seem clear that Gabriel was a name for an angel. Furthermore, this would indicate that angels at times take on appearances similar to men. This was the case, for example, when the angels came to visit Abraham and Lot in Genesis 18 and 19.

This same angel named Gabriel will appear again later in 9:21. And an angel by the name of Gabriel also spoke to reveal the message from God to Zechariah, the father of John the Baptist (Luke 1:19), and to Mary announcing that she would be the mother of Jesus by a miraculous conception (Luke 1:26). So Gabriel appears to have a role as a messenger at special times.

This shows us that an explanation will be forthcoming to help Daniel (and thereby to help us) understand the significance of the vision that Daniel had seen.

8:17-19 – As Gabriel approached, Daniel fell on his face in fear. But Gabriel told him to understand that the vision referred to the time of the end. Daniel was in a deep sleep, but Gabriel touched him and stood him up and said he would make known what would happen in the latter time of indignation at the appointed time of the end.

Gabriel then approached Daniel, but Daniel was so afraid that he fell on his face. Gabriel informed Daniel that he should understand that the vision referred to the time of the end. As Gabriel spoke, Daniel was in a deep sleep with his face to the ground (as in a faint or a swoon), then Gabriel touched him and stood him up right. And he informed Daniel that he was making known what would happen in the latter time of the indignation at the appointed time of the end.

So here we come to the explanation that was given to Daniel. These things would be fulfilled in the time of the end at a later time of indignation. There appears to be no reason to believe this is the final end of time, but to a time when God's indignation would come to a climax.

Hailey explains that Alexander and his successors devotedly advocated Greek philosophy and culture. The Jewish people may have become too influenced by false religious concepts so that God once again determined to punish them. When God's indignation reached the point that He determined to bring punishment, then He allowed the suffering described in these verses.

8:20-22 – The ram with the two horns referred to the kings of Media and Persia, and the male goat referred to the kingdom of Greece. The large horn between the eyes of the goat was its first king. That horn broke and four horns stood in its place referring to four kingdoms that would arise from Greece but lacking the power of the first king.

Then Gabriel gave a very clear and specific explanation of the vision. The ram represented the kingdom of the Medes and Persians. Its two horns represented the kings of those two people: one horn represented the king of Media and the other horn represented the king of Persia.

So, as we have discussed earlier, indeed the horns did represent kings. Gabriel did not expressly state it here, but the fact that one horn was higher than the other would imply that one kingdom (Persia) was more influential than the other (the Medes).

Then Gabriel said that the male goat in the vision represented the kingdom of Greece. And again the large horn between its eyes represented a king. It was the first king of the kingdom, which history tells us would be Alexander the Great (while he was not chronologically the first king of Greece, he was the first king of the Grecian Empire and the first in the sense of preeminence).

The fact that the horn would be broken refers to the fact that Alexander the Great would die, and his kingdom would be replaced by four kingdoms. None of those kingdoms, however, would have the power of the original kingdom.

Indeed, history records that this is exactly what happened. The Persians attempted repeatedly to invade and conquer Greece during the height of the Persian Empire. However, the Greeks defeated the Persians in two major battles: Marathon in 490 BC and a later sea battle near Salamis.

Finally, when Alexander the Great became king, he took the offensive and invaded the territory that had been held by the Persians, eventually conquering their entire territory. This also involved several major victories, one at the river Granicus (334 BC), another at Issus (333 BC), and one at Arbela (331 BC)

However, Alexander died at a very young age. Following his death, the territory he had conquered was divided into four sections: (1) Macedonia and Greece under Cassander, (2) Thrace and Asia Minor extending as far as India ruled by Lysimachus, (3) Syria and Babylon under the Seleucids, and (4) Egypt under Ptolemy. (At one point there were more than four divisions, but they soon narrowed down to three which were the only ones of significance historically.) The last two were of special interest to the Jews since Palestine was between Syria and Egypt.

The information given here is amazing. The passage predicts, even while Babylon still existed as the dominant Empire of the world, that it would be replaced by the kingdom of the Medes and Persians, which are here specifically named. That kingdom would in turn be defeated and replaced by the kingdom of Greece, which again is specifically named.

The earlier prophecies in chapters 2 and 7 had identified subsequent empires but without naming them. Here we find them specifically named years before they came to power. And not only are they named, but the destiny of the kingdom of Greece is specifically stated to be broken into four kingdoms. History records that Alexander died without an heir. As a result, his kingdom was divided among four of his generals.

So accurate are these predictions that skeptics deny that Daniel could have written these prophecies during the kingdom of Babylon. However, what we really have is amazing evidence of God's ability to foreknow the future and to foretell it through His prophets. Regardless of whether or not we understand all the specific details of every vision, there can be no gainsaying the overwhelming fact that Daniel revealed this information so specifically long before it occurred.

8:23-25 – Toward the end of their kingdom, when transgressors reached their fullness, a fierce and sinister king would arise. He would have great power, but not his own power. He would cause great destruction of the holy people. Deceit would prosper under his rule, and he would exalt himself. He would even rise against the Prince of princes, but he would be broken without human means.

In the latter time of these kings, transgressors would reach fullness. (Note that this is not the latter days, as in the reference to the New Testament period of the Messiah, but to the latter time in the kingdom to which the prophecy refers.) Then a fierce king would arise who understood sinister schemes. He would work by means of cunning and deceit (hypocrisy, deceitful words, etc.). He would have great power, but it would not be his own power. And he would cause great destruction, destroying the mighty and also the holy people (this refers to righteous "people," not to angels as some have claimed.)

But in all this he would thrive and prosper. He would exalt himself in his heart and destroy many people. The reference to destroying many in their prosperity appears, according to most translations, to mean that he brought punishment upon them while they were living in security and apparent prosperity. He would even rise against the Prince of princes, but in the end he would fall, but not by human means.

Gabriel does not tell us specifically who this king would be. But based on the previous information given in the vision, it appears that he would be the one who would cause the daily sacrifices to be taken away and the sanctuary to be trampled under foot for two thousand three hundred days, then the sanctuary would be cleansed as in verses 13,14.

Commentators generally conclude that the king to which this refers was Antiochus IV Epiphanes, king of Syria beginning in 175 BC. (Foy Wallace in *God's Prophetic Word* indicates that it refers to the Roman Empire, but I fail to see how this grew out of the Greek Empire as described in verses 9-12.)

Antiochus was determined to spread Greek philosophy and culture, but was convinced that Jewish religion and culture had to be destroyed to accomplish this. Possessing the characteristics described in these verses, he attacked Jewish religion. Historical records, including the books of the Maccabees, state that he was assisted in this by compromising high priests Jason and Menelaus.

We should note here the danger of the influences of society on God's people. In far too many cases the Jewish people allowed Greek philosophy and culture to influence them away from God's word. They cooperated with the evil forces around them rather than resisting them as they ought to have done. This may well happen today with the secularization and materialism that surrounds God's people. Far too often we go along with the world rather than combating it.

Harkrider says regarding Antiochus:

> "When he conquered Jerusalem, he set up an image in the temple, offered swine flesh upon the altar, and encouraged the Greek soldiers to commit fornication in the temple itself. And he forbade the Jews to circumcise their children, to keep the Sabbath, or even to possess a copy of the Scriptures." (Harkrider, page 43; See also 1 Maccabees 1:54-62)

This was a judgment on Israel, but it lasted only for a limited time and then ended. It is unclear whether the twenty-three hundred days is meant to be taken literally or symbolically. The vision has many symbols, but the explanation is in many ways highly literal. Keil & Delitzsch conclude that the number is effectively symbolic. However, Harkrider points out that the actual time of persecution lasted about six years, which would fit the number if it was literal.

In the end, Antiochus died, but not by war or physical attack from any people. Apparently he died from disease or accident. Some think he suffered madness. Others claim he died from grief because of military defeats.

8:26,27 – Daniel was then told that the vision was true, but he should seal it up because it referred to many days in the future. Daniel was so overwhelmed that he fainted and was sick for days, then finally he arose and went about the king's business. He was astonished by the vision but no one understood it.

Daniel was then told that the vision was true – that is, it would surely come to pass. But it would not happen for many days in the future, so he should seal it up. This is translated to seal it up (NKJV, ESV, NRSV) or to shut it up (KJV, ASV, MLV). But the NASB says to keep it secret.

This may mean that he was not to reveal the information right away because the fulfillment was not close at hand. But it seems more likely to me that this relates to the New Testament concept of a mystery. Paul often refers to the gospel as a mystery (Ephesians 3:3-5), not in the sense that it could never be understood, but in the sense that the meaning was not clearly revealed until the time of the complete revelation of the New Testament. So a prophecy, like the one Daniel received here, may be sealed, not in the sense that no one else could read it, but in the sense that it would not be understood until a time of greater revelation later. See also 1 Peter 1:9-12. See notes on 12:4.

This was the end of the vision as the information was given to Daniel. He was so amazed and troubled by what he had seen, that he fainted and was sick for days. Finally he was able to once again go about his work on the king's business. The vision had astonished him, but no one understood it.

Daniel 9

Chapter 9 – Daniel's Confession and the Vision of Seventy Weeks

> **Daniel's Confession; Vision of Seventy Weeks**
> Daniel understood that the Babylonian captivity was about to end.
> He confessed to God the sins of the people in contrast to the mercy of God.
> He called upon God to turn away his anger and forgive.
> An angel told Daniel that seventy weeks were determined to finish the transgression, make an end of sins, make reconciliation for iniquity, bring in everlasting righteousness, seal up vision and prophecy, to anoint the Most Holy.

9:1,2 – In the first year of Darius, son of Ahasuerus, Daniel recognized from the prophecies of Jeremiah that Jerusalem would be desolate for seventy years.

The events in this chapter took place in the first year of the reign of Darius, son of Ahasuerus, who was of the lineage of the Medes. This Darius was king over the realm of the Chaldeans. It was during the reign of this king that Daniel was one of the three governors over the kingdom (chapter 6). Yet despite his high position and great responsibilities, not only did he find time to pray, but he also studied the Scriptures (verse 2). This is a useful lesson to us regarding the use of our time.

Based on his understanding of the books, specifically the message of God through Jeremiah the prophet, Daniel realized that the number of years Jerusalem would remain desolate was seventy years. That is, God had prophesied that the people would be in captivity for their sins seventy years. That time was just about completed, which led Daniel to make the plea described in this chapter.

These prophecies of Jeremiah are recorded in several places:

Jeremiah 25:11,12 – And this whole land shall be a desolation and an astonishment, and these nations shall serve the king of Babylon seventy years. "Then it will come to pass, when seventy years are completed, that I will punish the king of Babylon and that nation, the land of the Chaldeans, for their iniquity," says the LORD; "and I will make it a perpetual desolation."

Jeremiah 29:10 – For thus says the LORD: After seventy years are completed at Babylon, I will visit you and perform My good word toward you, and cause you to return to this place.

2 Chronicles 36:21 – To fulfill the word of the LORD by the mouth of Jeremiah, until the land had enjoyed her Sabbaths. As long as she lay desolate she kept Sabbath, to fulfill seventy years.

Notice important lessons we can learn here about the value of Scripture. We can learn that the written records of the prophets – Jeremiah in this case – were circulated and known among God's people hundreds of years before the time of Christ. Furthermore, they were used as an authoritative means of learning and understanding the will of God. Daniel respected the written record of the message of Jeremiah as being "the word of the Lord." We should do the same with the Scriptures that have come to us.

9:3-5 – Then Daniel prayed to God with fasting, sackcloth, and ashes, and confession to the awesome God who keeps His covenant toward those who love Him and keep His commandments. He confessed that the people had sinned and rebelled by departing from His precepts and judgments.

Daniel then prayed to God and confessed the sins the people. He made request with prayer and supplication, with fasting, sackcloth, and ashes: all indications of great sorrow and repentance. He described God as the great and awesome God who keeps His covenant and mercy with those who love Him and keep His commandments. This characteristic of God was important to Daniel's request, since he was about to appeal to God for mercy.

He then confessed that the people had sinned and committed iniquity. They had done wickedly and rebelled. In particular, they had departed from God's precepts and judgments. These were the reasons why they had gone into captivity in the first place. Daniel was recognizing and acknowledging the justice of God in punishing the people by sending them into captivity. This was his introduction to the request he hoped to make.

When God had warned Israel that He would send them into captivity if they persisted in their sins, especially in idolatry, He had also instructed them that they could return from captivity if they would truly repent and confess their sins. See Leviticus 26:40-42; 1 Kings

8:47-49. This is what Daniel set about to do on behalf of the people. See also Nehemiah chapter 9.

9:6-8 – The people had not obeyed the prophets who spoke in the name of God to their rulers, their ancestors, and all the people. God is righteous. But shame of face belonged to the people whom God had driven into foreign countries because of their unfaithfulness and their sins.

Daniel continued describing the sins of the people saying that they had not obeyed the warnings of the prophets who spoke in the name of God. The prophets had warned the rulers, previous generations, and all the people. They knew the consequences of disobedience, or there was no excuse for them if they did not know.

So God was righteous. By driving the people into foreign lands, He had done exactly what He had said He would do if they were unfaithful. But the people deserved to be ashamed because of their sins and their unfaithfulness toward God.

Daniel is here recognizing that, even though the people had been sent to captivity, yet God was just and fair in doing this. He had warned the people repeatedly, but the people had ignored the warnings, including the warnings from the prophets. Prophets had admonished the people's rulers, and they had warned the people. Even in past generations, prophets had spoken warnings. But the people refused to listen, so God was just, whereas the people deserved to be ashamed of their conduct.

9:9-11 – Though the people had rebelled against God, yet He is a God of mercy and forgiveness. The people had not obeyed God to walk in the laws revealed by His prophets. All Israel had transgressed the law. So the curse written in the Law of Moses had been poured out on them because of their sins.

Daniel continued to enlarge on the sins of the people. But he repeatedly acknowledged, in contrast to the sins of the people, that God was merciful and forgiving despite the rebellion of the people. Of course, as his prayer proceeded he hoped to call upon God to be forgiving.

Again, he emphasized that the people had not obeyed the voice of God by walking in the laws that had been taught them by God's servants the prophets. Instead, all Israel had transgressed God's law and departed by not obeying the voice of God. This was why they were suffering the consequences of the curse and the oath written in the Law of Moses. They had sinned, so the punishment had been poured out on them.

As discussed earlier, this warning of consequences had been revealed as far back as Moses. See Leviticus 26:14-46; Deuteronomy 27:15-26; 28:15-68; 29:20-29; 30:17-19; 32:19-42.

9:12-14 – God confirmed His words by bringing upon Jerusalem a disaster such as had never been done under heaven. This had been written in the Law of Moses, but the people had not prayed to God that they might turn from iniquity and understand the truth. So God was righteous in all that He does though the people had not obeyed.

God had predicted in the Law of Moses the disaster that would come upon the people, as we have discussed in previous verses. Yet despite these warnings from God, the people had not prayed to God and had not turned from sin to truly realize and appreciate the truth.

So, God confirmed His word that He spoke against the people and against their judges by bringing on Jerusalem a disaster so great that nothing like it had ever been done under heaven. Surely other nations had suffered great disasters at the hands of their enemies, but this had happened to the chosen nation who were the people of the true God. God remembered the disaster that He promised to bring, and He had fulfilled His word.

This did not mean God was cruel or unfair. On the contrary, He was righteous. He had warned the people how to avoid these consequences, but His righteous nature could not lead Him to ignore sin. The people did not obey, so God kept His promise and brought disaster upon them.

We should remember, as Daniel observed here, that God is always fair and upright in His judgments. He never punishes those who are unworthy of punishment, yet He is always a God of mercy to those who are willing to repent and confess their sins. As He did with Israel and Judah, so God will also punish us and any others in our own day if we do not repent of our sins. And when He does so, it will be just and fair, because God is always righteous in His judgments.

9:15,16 – God had brought Israel out of the land of Egypt and made Himself a name, but the people had sinned and done wickedly. So Daniel prayed that God would be so righteous as to turn away His anger from Jerusalem. Because of their sins Jerusalem and the people were a reproach to all around.

Here Daniel comes to the specific request toward which he had been moving throughout this prayer. He had confessed the sins of the people. He had acknowledged that God was righteous and upright to punish the people because they had persisted in their sins despite His warnings. God was just and upright, but the problem was caused by the people who had sinned and would not repent. So God had sent them into captivity as He had repeatedly promised He would do.

But now the seventy years as prophesied by Jeremiah had reached its fulfillment. And God had punished the people as He said that He would. So Daniel's purpose in the prayer was to request that God would now show mercy on the people and bring their captivity to an end.

He reminded God that, by means of His great power, He had brought the people out of Egypt from their captivity. Of course, God knew this and did not need to be reminded. But Daniel was acknowledging what God had done and was now requesting that once again God would show mercy on the people and deliver them from captivity.

He said the people had become a reproach to all those around. This, of course, was true. This was part of what God had predicted would happen as a result of their sins. Daniel was now requesting that the reproach be taken away by a return from captivity.

9:17-19 – So Daniel called God for His own sake to cause His face to shine on His desolate sanctuary. He urged God to incline His ear and open His eyes and see the desolation of the city that was called by His name. He asked, not because the people were so righteous, but because God was merciful. So he urged God to forgive the city and people called by His name.

So Daniel reached the climax of his prayer as he asked God to hear his prayer and his supplication and for the Lord's sake to cause His face to shine on His sanctuary, which had been made desolate. He urged God to incline His ear and listen and open His eyes and see the desolation being suffered by the city that was called by His name.

He did not ask God to bless the people because they were so righteous, but he asked because he knew that God was a God of mercy. So he called upon God to hear and to forgive. He urged God to act without delay for the sake of God, because the city and the people were called by the name of God.

The clear import of Daniel's request was for God to forgive the people who were suffering so in captivity because of God's punishments for their sin. He did not deny that the punishment was deserved. On the contrary, he acknowledged that God was right and just in punishing the people for their sins. But the request was for the God to now forgive the people and bring the punishment to an end.

Furthermore, the request was not based on the fact the people now were so good that they deserved to be forgiven. Rather, the request was based on the fact that God is so good that He is merciful and will bring forgiveness on those who repent and ask.

And furthermore, the request was not so much because the people deserved it as because God Himself was being reproached by the conditions of the people. They were His people and Jerusalem was His city. The captivity of the people and desolation of the city brought reproach upon God Himself. So Daniel urged God to act for His own sake as well as for the sake of the people.

There is much for us to learn here about prayer. We should not pray for God to bless us because we deserve it. We should ask with humility trusting in the goodness of God, not in our own goodness. And we should always seek what would honor God, not just what would please us.

Furthermore, we should learn lessons from the great respect with which Daniel addressed God. His prayer expressed the greatness of God and the unworthiness of people. Our prayers should exult God and demonstrate our own humility, which in turn means we should speak with the utmost respect for the Ruler of the universe.

9:20-23 – As Daniel was praying and confessing, Gabriel flew swiftly and arrived about the time of the evening offering. Because Daniel was greatly loved, he had been instructed at the beginning of the supplication to come and help Daniel understand the vision.

So even as Daniel was praying and confessing his sins and the sins of the people in making his supplication to God on behalf of Jerusalem, Gabriel arrived. This was the same Gabriel who had spoken to Daniel to explain a previous vision (8:16). He arrived about the time of the evening offering having flown swiftly.

Gabriel informed Daniel that he had come to give Daniel the skill to understand. In fact, at the very beginning of Daniel's supplication, the command went forth. So Gabriel had come to give explanation to Daniel because he was greatly beloved. Gabriel then proceeded to urge Daniel to consider the matter and understand the vision.

The reference to the evening sacrifice here does not indicate that the sacrifices were being offered at the time of Daniel's writing. Those sacrifices had ceased when the temple in Jerusalem had been destroyed early in the life of Daniel. And furthermore, Daniel had been taken into captivity in Babylon, so he certainly had no way to participate in the evening sacrifice.

The purpose of the reference to the evening sacrifice was simply to identify the time of day when Daniel received this revelation. Though the sacrifices no longer were being offered, all Jews would understand the time of day when they traditionally had been offered.

9:24,25 – *Seventy weeks were determined to finish the transgression, to make an end of sins, to make reconciliation for iniquity, to bring in everlasting righteousness, to seal up vision and prophecy, and to anoint the Most Holy. So from the going forth of the command to restore and build Jerusalem until Messiah the Prince would be sixty-nine weeks. The street and the wall would be built again even in troublesome times.*

Gabriel revealed by way of prediction that a period of seventy weeks had been assigned to finish the transgression, make an end of sins, make reconciliation for iniquity, bring in everlasting righteousness, seal up vision and prophecy, and anoint the Most Holy. So, from the going forth of the command to restore and build Jerusalem until Messiah the Prince, would be seven weeks and sixty-two weeks. The street and the wall would be built again even in troublesome times.

This is without doubt one of the most difficult parts of the book of Daniel: some say it is one of the most difficult sections in the Bible. One reason, however, why the passage is so difficult is that men have twisted it to formulate all kinds of speculative theories in order to support their doctrines which cannot be supported here or elsewhere in Scripture.

Gabriel revealed to Daniel some very specific events that would take place in a period described as seventy weeks. Doubtless Daniel did not understand what events were being prophesied, nor would we without the fulfillment of these events and the explanations we have in the New Testament.

Perhaps the most difficult part of the prophecy relates to the time periods involved. Gabriel refers to seven weeks, then sixty-two weeks, then a final week, totaling seventy weeks. Commentators have struggled mightily trying to give specific rules or explanations to define how these time periods would be measured.

Commentators – especially premillennial commentators – have a heyday speculating on the fulfillment of these predictions. They come up with all kinds of imaginary ideas. But aside from the fact that they cannot prove these speculations, the main problem is that they contradict many other clear and important doctrines taught elsewhere in Scripture.

See our notes on chapter 2 for a refutation of many of the errors of premillennialism. We will not put forth much effort here to further refute those errors but will attempt to understand that the passage does teach.

To learn more about the errors of the premillennial views we urge you to study our free articles on that subject on our Bible study web site at www.gospelway.com/instruct (see the section about "Man").

Remember that the prophets who revealed Old Testament predictions often themselves did not understand the fulfillment of their predictions. The meaning of the prophecies became clear only after the prophecies were fulfilled, when the prophesied events had occurred and fuller revelation was given in the New Testament. Until that time, the meaning of the Old Testament prophecy was a mystery. This is clearly stated in Ephesians 3:3-5 and 1 Peter 1:10-12.

So I would approach this prophecy from Daniel by setting aside for now the meaning of the time periods and looking instead at the *events* that are mentioned. Let us see if we can understand the meaning of these events in light of subsequent history and especially in light of New Testament teaching. If we can achieve a fairly good grasp on the events, then we will work back from there to understand the timing described.

The command to restore and rebuild Jerusalem

The events related to Daniel's people and the holy city. That must surely refer to the nation of Israel (Judah) and Jerusalem (Nehemiah 11:1). The events begin with the going forth of the command to restore and rebuild Jerusalem and they continue until Messiah the Prince.

This part should be fairly straightforward. Daniel had gone into captivity when Nebuchadnezzar had attacked Judah, ultimately resulting in the destruction of Jerusalem. In this chapter Daniel had been praying for God to forgive the people and restore them to Canaan as God had revealed through Jeremiah that He would do after they had been in captivity seventy years. Daniel had concluded that the time had come, and that was the subject of his prayer.

So it appears clear that Gabriel's response is promising to Daniel that the city would be rebuilt. The street and the wall would be repaired, even though this would be done during troublesome times. This was fulfilled as revealed in the books of Ezra and Nehemiah.

However, the prophecy proceeds to describe the ultimate destruction of the city of Jerusalem many years in the future. So whereas Gabriel predicts that the city would be rebuilt, he also predicts that it would ultimately be destroyed. Following that, it would no longer have any special purpose in God's plan.

Daniel's prophecy was given to him in the first year of Darius the Mede (9:1,2; 5:31). This would also be the same time that, in fulfillment to God's promise, Cyrus gave the degree for the people to return to Jerusalem and rebuild the city and the temple (Ezra 1:1-4; 2 Chronicles 36:22,23; Isaiah 44:26-28; 45:1-4). Historical evidence indicates that this would have occurred about 538 BC. This fulfilled prophecy of Jeremiah (25:11,12; 29:10) and of Isaiah (44:28; 45:1-7,13).

Zerubbabel led the first group to return (536 BC). Then Ezra led a group who returned to rebuild the temple (458 BC). And Nehemiah led a group that returned to rebuild the walls (444 BC). This was accomplished despite severe opposition from the people of the land as revealed in the books of Ezra and Nehemiah. This is the beginning of Gabriel's prophecy.

The Messiah the Prince

At the other end of the time period would be the coming of the Messiah who was also described as the Prince. This also should be straightforward. The New Testament clearly reveals that the Messiah was Jesus Christ, Christ being the New Testament word for Messiah. (Matthew 16:16; 26:63,64; John 6:69; 11:27; 20:30,31; Acts 8:37; 17:3).

So the coming of Jesus related to the end of the time period. From the going forth of the command to rebuild Jerusalem until the Messiah would be seven weeks followed by sixty-two weeks. Other events would then come in the final week as described in subsequent verses.

To finish the transgression, to make an end of sins, to make reconciliation for iniquity, to bring in everlasting righteousness

These expressions seem to me all to refer to the same idea, describing one of the most important things to happen as a result of this period of seventy weeks. Transgression would be finished and sins would be ended, not in the sense that they would never happen again, but in the sense that there would be reconciliation to bring a permanent forgiveness. The result would be everlasting righteousness.

This would especially include the sins of the people of Judah which Daniel had confessed in verses 9-11. These would be finished even though the nation would no longer have any favored status with God. They would be finished by means of salvation under the gospel.

In the way of contrast, under the Old Testament the people were commanded to offer sacrifices for sins, but those sacrifices never really finished or ended the sins. They did not bring in everlasting righteousness because the sins would be remembered again. The sins were not so put away as to never again be held against the people, but they would be remembered again every year. See Hebrews 10:1-18. Compare 1 John 2:1,2; Acts 22:16.

However, when Jesus came and offered the ultimate and true sacrifice for sins, iniquity would be reconciled and transgression and sins would be finished or ended so that they would never again be held against the one who was forgiven. The resulting righteousness would be everlasting in the sense that they would lead to everlasting life because the sins would never again be held against the sinner.

All this happened, of course, through the Christ who offered the perfect sacrifice at His crucifixion. We now can look back at this and see the fulfillment, though it is doubtful that Daniel would have understood it. Isaiah 53 describes this concept as clearly as any place in the Old Testament (see also Jeremiah 31:34). It is repeatedly described in the New Testament.

See Matthew 1:21; 26:28; 20:28; Ephesians 1:7; 1 Peter 1:18,19; 2:24; Hebrews 2:9,14,15; Revelation 1:5; 5:9; 1 Timothy 2:4-6; Isaiah 53:5-12; 1 Corinthians 15:3; John 1:29; Hebrews 7:27; 8:12; 9:12-14,24-28; 10:9-13; 13:20,21; Romans 3:21,22; 5:6-11; 2 Corinthians 5:14,15,18-21; Colossians 1:20-22; Philippians 3:9.

To seal up vision and prophecy

In Daniel 8:26 Daniel was told to seal up a vision because it referred to many days in the future. In Revelation 22:10 John was told not to seal up a prophecy because the time was at hand. These examples may indicate that sealing up a vision or prophecy might refer simply to ending or closing it.

In Revelation 10:4 John had heard something but was told to seal up what he heard – i.e., he was not to write it and as a result people would not know it. In Revelation 5 no one could read the message in the book in God's hand (until Jesus unsealed it), because it was sealed with seven seals. But how would such an idea fit the context here?

Others have suggested that sealing up the vision and prophecy simply means the fulfillment of it or achieving its end. An official message was sealed when it had been completed or come to an end. Surely numerous prophecies were fulfilled by the coming of the Messiah and the sacrifice He offered for sins. If that is the meaning, that would certainly make sense. But it would be a different meaning of the expression "seal up" from the meaning that appears to me to be used elsewhere.

It seems to me that the meaning here refers primarily to the fact that the contents of the message would be hidden or secret or a "mystery" so that no could understand it until some future time. See notes on Daniel 12:4 for a fuller explanation.

To anoint the Most Holy

Another major purpose accomplished in this period would be the anointing of the Most Holy. This could refer to the Most Holy person or the Most Holy Place. The obvious significance described in the New Testament refers to the anointment of Jesus as the Christ. Christ means anointed one. Jesus was anointed as our spiritual king, priest, and prophet. Psalm 45:7; 2:2; Hebrews 1:8,9; Isaiah 61:1; Acts 4:26,27; John 1:41; Luke 4:18.

Furthermore, Jesus is repeatedly called the holy One: Mark 1:24; Luke 1:35; 4:34; Acts 3:14; Hebrews 7:26; Revelation 3:7.

This would fit the prophecy as we have described because the seventy weeks would continue until the Messiah, the Anointed One (verse 25).

9:26,27 – After sixty-two weeks Messiah would be cut off but not for Himself. The people of the prince who is to come will destroy the city and the sanctuary. It will end with a flood; and till the end of the war desolations are determined. Then he will confirm a covenant with many for one week, but in the middle of the week He will end sacrifice and offering. On the wing of abominations one will make it desolate even until the consummation, which is determined, is poured out on the desolate.

The sixty-two weeks would lead up to the time when the Messiah would be cut off, but would not be cut off for Himself. The prince would have a covenant with many for a week, but in the middle of the week, he would end sacrifice and offering. Someone would make desolation on the wing of abominations until the consummation which has been determined would be poured out on the desolate.

Messiah shall be cut off, but not for Himself

The sixty-two weeks had been described in verses 24,25 as a period following seven weeks. After this period of sixty-two weeks, the Messiah would be cut off but not for Himself. So the prophecy is still referring to the Messiah, the Prince (verse 25).

The phrase "cut off" is sometimes used to refer to the death penalty or severe penalty for sin (Leviticus 7:20,21,25,27; 17:4,9,10,14). The fact that He would be cut off surely refers to the crucifixion or death of Christ (Isaiah 53:8).

He would die, but not for Himself. That is, He was not dying because He deserved to die but He was dying for the benefit of others. Jesus died as a sacrifice for our sins as described in many Scriptures, especially Isaiah chapter 53. This is how He would accomplish everlasting righteousness and the end of sin as described in verse 23. See verses listed above.

(Some translations say He would be cut off and would have nothing. It is true that, at the time He was crucified, Jesus possessed nothing in this physical realm, nor did he even have a kingdom yet. In any case, the prophecy is true. But it is uncertain which is the proper translation.)

A further confirmation that this prophecy is fulfilled in the time period surrounding the life and death of Jesus and the events following, is found in passages like Acts 3:21-24. There Peter explained that all the prophets spoke regarding the time of Jesus' life and death and the surrounding events. Of course, not every prophecy concerned those events, but the point is that the prophets commonly spoke of those events. So, it is reasonable to conclude that we have an example of such a prophecy here in Daniel 9.

And the people of the prince who is to come shall destroy the city and the sanctuary. The end of it shall be with a flood, and till the end of the war desolations are determined.

After the completion of the sixty-two weeks (which follow the seven weeks), not only will the Messiah be cut off, but also the city and the sanctuary will be destroyed. The end of it will come with a flood and will involve a war. Desolations are determined to continue until the end of the war. The reference to a flood would imply the overwhelming nature of the destruction (compare similar language in Isaiah 8:5-8).

As we have seen, the context shows that the city refers to Jerusalem and the sanctuary refers to the temple. So this is a prophecy of the destruction of Jerusalem and the temple. It surely does not refer to the destruction brought upon Jerusalem by the Babylonians under Nebuchadnezzar, since that had already occurred. So the fulfillment must refer to the destruction of Jerusalem in 70 A.D. This occurred sometime relatively soon after the Messiah was cut off.

In Matthew 24 Jesus prophesied at great length the suffering and hardships that would relate to the destruction of Jerusalem and the temple. Prophecies often refer to such sufferings as desolation, especially when brought about by a judgment from God upon the evils of a nation or city. Note that the terms "desolate" or "desolation" are used several times in verses 26,27. Jesus specifically used this term to refer to the end of the Jewish nation in Matthew 23:38 just before He prophesied the destruction of the temple in Matthew chapter 24.

This destruction would be brought about by the people of the prince. So the question is: What prince and what people are referred to here? The Messiah was called the Prince in verse 25. And there is a sense in which Christ brought about the destruction of Jerusalem in 70 A.D. It was a punishment from God brought upon the people in the city because of their rejection of the will of God and especially their rejection of Jesus as the Messiah.

However, the passage says that the destruction would be caused by the people of the prince, rather than specifically by the prince himself. I can think of no way that the people of Jesus Christ caused the destruction of Jerusalem in any way that makes sense as a fulfillment of the prophecy. They did not in any way cause or participate in the war referred to here.

Furthermore, the NKJV does not capitalize the word "prince" here, which would indicate that the translators at least did not believe that it referred to the Messiah. So the reference would be to the people of some other prince who caused the destruction. The reasonable answer here would be the Roman armies that destroyed the city and the temple in 70 A.D. The prince who led them was Titus, son of Vespasian, who was the Emperor of Rome.

Then he shall confirm a covenant with many for one week.

The meaning here seems more difficult to me. Who is the one who confirms a covenant, and what is the covenant? We have two different princes being referred to: the Messiah and the prince whose people would destroy Jerusalem.

If the Roman ruler is the prince who made the covenant, then the covenant may simply have been an arrangement by which the people could have peace with the Roman government. If this arrangement continued for a while, then the destruction of the temple by Titus would fulfill the cutting off of the sacrifice and offering.

On the other hand, Jesus surely made a covenant with the people, since the New Testament is referred to repeatedly, especially in the book of Hebrews, as a covenant. However, the passage does not say that He would make a covenant but that He would "confirm" a covenant. This could very likely refer to the covenant God made with Abraham. Jesus confirmed this by offering the sacrifice which was the blessing upon all nations as promised to Abraham (Acts 3:25; Galatians 3:16,17; Luke 1:2,52).

Jesus confirmed the covenant made with Abraham so that many would benefit from it. The one week must have begun at the coming of Jesus and continued till the destruction of Jerusalem in A.D. 70.

But in the middle of the week He shall bring an end to sacrifice and offering.

In the middle of the week of the covenant (some translations say "midst" and others say "half"), he shall bring an end to sacrifice and offering. But who is it that causes this end, and when did it occur? The ruler of the Romans did so in the sense that he brought about the destruction of the temple, thereby ending the sacrifices.

However, it can also be said that the Messiah ended the sacrifices and offerings. Again, the NKJV seems to think this is the meaning, since it capitalizes the word "He." Jesus ended sacrifice and offerings by making them unnecessary. His death was the one sacrifice to save all people for all time to come so that from that time on there was no longer need for animal sacrifices. He ended them in the sense of making them no longer needed or useful. See Hebrews 9:11-17; 10:1-18.

This latter view seems to me to make more sense. Jesus the Messiah would be cut off in the middle of the week, but the week itself would end at the destruction of Jerusalem. The offering of the sacrifices would not actively cease until the destruction of Jerusalem. But it was Jesus' death on the cross that brought an end to them in the sense of making them unnecessary.

In any case, the end of the sacrifice and offering was permanent. There was no reason nor any means by which it could be restored. The death of Jesus removed any purpose for animal sacrifices, and the destruction of Jerusalem ended the means by which they were offered. There was no further a temple nor priesthood to offer them. From that time till now the sacrifice and offering have ceased.

And on the wing of abominations shall be one who makes desolate, even until the consummation, which is determined, is poured out on the desolate.

In the destruction of Jerusalem and the temple, there would be one who makes desolate. This would continue to be poured out on those who are desolate until the consummation or the end that has been determined. These are described as coming on the wing of abominations.

This meaning might be especially difficult. And many speculations have been suggested, especially by premillennial speculators. However, there is no need for speculation since Jesus Himself cleared up the meaning of the prophecy when He Himself prophesied the destruction of Jerusalem.

In Jesus' prophecy, as described in Mark 13:14, He refers to the "abomination of desolation" that was spoken of by Daniel (see Daniel 9:27; 11:31; and 12:11). But fortunately the parallel in Luke 21:20 settles without doubt and for all time what this means. The passage is clearly parallel to Matthew 24:15 and Mark 13:14, since all the passages say that this is the thing which, when you see it, it is the sign to flee and woe to those who are pregnant, etc.

Luke 21:20 shows that the "abomination of desolation" refers to armies surrounding Jerusalem that would cause her desolation. "Desolation" is a word that is often used by the Old Testament prophets to describe the destruction of a nation or city. In Matthew 23:38 Jesus addressed Jerusalem and said that her house was left desolate. What made her desolate? The Roman armies surrounded the city and eventually destroyed the city, the temple, and thousands of people.

That this is in fact the "abomination of desolation" is interestingly confirmed by Josephus, the Jewish historian. McGarvey quote Josephus as follows: "Daniel also wrote concerning the Roman government, that our country should be made desolate by them" (Antiquities, B. x, ch. xi, Paragraph 7).

So the prophecy of Jesus himself makes clear that the one who made it desolate – that is, "the abomination of desolation" – refers to the armies surrounding Jerusalem that would bring about her destruction. Therefore, it refers to the Roman armies under a Roman ruler. That clarifies the significance of Daniel's prophecy here.

(There is alternative explanation here. King suggests that the abomination refers to the sins of the Jewish people. The coming of the desolation was a punishment that came upon the people for their sins. But even in this view the desolation is still the destruction of Jerusalem.)

So, based on the events that Daniel prophesied in light of the fulfillment in the New Testament, it seems clear that **the seventy weeks represents the time from the command to restore the temple till the time the temple was destroyed in 70 A.D.**

The meaning of the weeks in Daniel's prophecy

The weeks are not literal, nor do they represent 490 years.

Observing the *fulfillment* of the **events** in Daniel's prophecy, as we have done, seems to me to clarify the meaning of the prophecy itself. Speculation is not needed in light of the clear record of Scripture and history. Some details may not be clear, but we have substantial evidence for the meaning of the main points of the prophecy.

The primary difficulty that remains relates to the number of weeks. We have seven weeks, then sixty-two weeks, then a final week, totaling "seventy weeks." Let us do what we can to unravel the meaning. I emphasize again that, in such a highly symbolic context, we must surely approach these numbers as symbols, not intended to be literal. Symbolic uses of time periods in prophecy are quite common.

In fact I know of no one, regardless of their views, who believes that the seventy weeks are literal weeks: i.e., four hundred ninety **days** or a little more than a year. No one believes these prophecies were all fulfilled within slightly over a literal year of Daniel's time. So we must look for a different meaning.

However, the footnotes in many translations show that the word which is here translated "weeks" simply means "sevens." It is translated "weeks." But it may simply refer to seven things according to context. This concept is confirmed by Brown-Driver-Briggs. However, this certainly does not appear to be a very common usage. In fact, this prophecy in Daniel 9 appears to be the only passage where it means other than a literal week.

Some believe that each day represents a year, so the seventy weeks refer to four hundred ninety years. Some insist that the four hundred ninety years is the literal approach to the passage, so they go to great lengths to try to establish events that literally fit four hundred ninety years. Frankly, I see no reason to insist that these would be literal years when we are dealing with such a highly symbolic prophecy.

So far as I can tell, there is no way that four hundred ninety years would fit the **events** that are prophesied. Others have tried to find various ways of assigning meaning to the weeks, but so far as I can tell all have been unsuccessful.

Consider some comments to this effect:

"There is no satisfactory proof in Dan. 9 that weeks of years are intended. It appears there is no way mathematically to fit these numbers into the major events of history without too much, or too short a time, between each event. We can determine the time span only by the events described." (Harkrider, page 47)

"...it has proven foolish to attempt to apply a literalistic approach to these numbers, however, taking them as weeks that somehow indicate an exact number of years. We have no interest in the pursuit of such 'number crunching' efforts. In our way of thinking the entire process loses the reader in a maze of mathematical possibilities, enters into the realm of rank speculation, and takes his mind off the main force of the passage. Rather, it is clear that we are dealing with an elaborate symbolism and the numbers are merely symbolic representations of blocks of time." (Daniel H King, *The Book of Daniel*, page 626)

"In light of the symbolic interpretation of Daniel's visions, it seems perfectly reasonable to believe that the seventy weeks are figurative also, and symbolize various periods of time in history that lay ahead for the Jewish people. ... The 'seventy weeks' symbolize the entire period from the Decree of Cyrus allowing the Jews to return to Jerusalem and rebuild the temple, to the destruction of Jerusalem by the Romans..." (Hailey, page 187)

Similar statements can be cited from other commentators. Remember that we know the fulfillment of the prophecy based on of the Scriptures and history. But this still leaves the problem of determining the symbolic meaning of the weeks.

The numbers seven and ten are important symbols, especially in prophecy.

The number seven is a highly symbolic number throughout Scripture. From the time of the creation a seven-day week has had special significance (Genesis 1,2). At the end of that seven days, God's work was complete and very good. So throughout the Scriptures the number seven often refers to that which is ***perfect or complete***. (See Genesis 4:15,24; Isaiah 30:26; Daniel 3:19; 4:23,25,32; Proverbs 6:31; Matthew 18:21; etc.)

So a week would symbolize completeness or finality or perfection. But we have here a period of seventy weeks, which multiplies the seven days in a week times seven weeks times ten: 7 x 7 x 10. The number ten is also often used in Scripture, especially prophecy, as a symbol of that which is complete. See Daniel 1:20; Genesis 31:7; Numbers 14:22; Nehemiah 4:12; Job 19:3.

So here we have the complete or perfect number seven multiplied times the complete number ten and then multiplied by the seven days in the week. The end result would multiply and thereby reemphasize the completeness of the time.

If this approach is correct, then the purpose of the seventy weeks symbolically is not to identify a literal length of time. Rather, the purpose is to emphasize the completeness of the time, so that the prophecy is predicting that **the purpose of God would be fully completed in the fullness of time**. This fits New Testament statements regarding the fact that the Messiah came in the fullness of time according to God's purpose (Galatians 4:4; Mark 1:15; Ephesians 1:10; Hebrews 9:10).

Nevertheless, the approach leaves a number of questions unanswered regarding the specific significance of the first seven weeks, then sixty-two weeks, then a final week. One suggestion is that the first seven weeks refer symbolically to the time period while Judah was returning from captivity and rebuilding the city and the temple in Jerusalem. Then the sixty-two weeks refers to the period from the completion of the rebuilding of the city to the coming of Christ. Then the final week refers to the period from the coming of Christ until the destruction of Jerusalem.

If this is correct, then Jesus' death would have occurred in the middle of the final week, and that death would have brought the end of sacrifice and offerings because they were no longer needed.

The symbolic significance of the number seven.

Phil Roberts published a study regarding the numerical symbolism of the seventy weeks (Florida College Annual Lectures 1986, reprinted in Homer Hailey's commentary on Daniel.) He points out that the seventy weeks is symbolic, not intended to be literal.

He emphasizes the significance of the number seven in regard to the week and the Sabbath day. The number seven symbolized completion or perfection based on the creation week, because at the end of the week everything God had made was very good: perfect and complete. So the number seven became a symbol for perfection and completion.

The Sabbath day had special significance to the nation of Israel (Exodus 31:13). In addition there were other sabbaths including the sabbath year, which involved a rest for the land every seventh year. There was also the Jubilee, which occurred the year after every seventh seven years, or forty-nine years (seven times seven). See Leviticus 25:1-34; 26:34; 2 Chronicles 36:21.

The Sabbath day symbolized two things to Israel: the **completion** of the creation (including God's rest on the seventh day) and also God's **deliverance** of Israel from Egyptian captivity (Exodus 20:11; Deuteronomy 5:15). So the Sabbath had a double meaning: rest and deliverance. This then symbolized Israel's entrance into rest when they entered into the land of Canaan after they were delivered from Egypt (Deuteronomy 12:9,10). This in turn became a symbol of our rest in heaven when we have been delivered from the bondage of sin (Hebrews 4:1-11).

So the number seven had symbolic significance to Israelites, not just as a symbol of completion or perfection, but also as a symbol of rest and deliverance. The number ten also symbolized completeness. The number seventy then would represent ten sevens, multiplying the concept of completeness and the concept of rest and deliverance. So, for example, Israel would be delivered and have rest after seventy years of Babylonian captivity.

The seventy weeks of Daniel 9 then multiplies the significance even more: ten sevens times seven days in each week equals four hundred ninety. Compare this to Jesus reference to 70×7 regarding forgiveness or deliverance from sin in Matthew 18:22. We all recognize this to be a symbolic number, not literal.

So the seventy weeks is symbolic, not intended to be literal. It symbolizes the period from the decree to rebuild the temple until the complete and perfect completion of God's plan to give men rest and deliverance from sin. That would include the sacrifice of Jesus and the fulfillment or end of God's purpose for the nation of Israel. The symbolic significance of the seventy weeks emphasizes, not a specific time period, but the completeness and perfection of God's development of His plan for man's salvation.

Wallace (in *God's Prophetic Word*) summarizes the fulfillment of Daniel 9 as follows**:

* Finish the transgression and make an end of sin – Hebrews 10:12; 8:12; Ephesians 2:15.

* Bring everlasting righteousness – Romans 3:21-31; 2 Corinthians 5:21.

* Reconciliation for iniquity – Colossians 1:20-22; Hebrews 2:17; Romans 5:6-10; Ephesians 2:11-18.

* Anoint the most Holy – Acts 4:26-27; Hebrews 1:8-9; Acts 2:25-36.

* The Messiah cut off – Isaiah 53:8; Acts 8:32-33.

* Destroy the city and sanctuary – Matthew 24:1-34.

* Covenant confirmed with many – Acts 10:34; Romans 9:30.

(** Additional references suggested by Josh Welsh)

Daniel 10

Daniel 10-12 – Vision in the Third Year of Cyrus

> **An Angel Appears to Give Daniel Information About the Future**
> A man/angel of amazing appearance came to Daniel.
> He would make Daniel understand events in the latter days.
> Daniel was left without strength but was given strength.

10:1-3 – In the third year of king Cyrus Daniel received a revelation to be fulfilled after a long time. It came while he was mourning and fasting, eating no pleasant food or wine or meat for three weeks.

This chapter begins the record of another revelation that Daniel received. This one was in the third year of Cyrus king of Persia. Daniel affirms that it was true and that he understood the message, but the time for it to be fulfilled was in the distant future (or "it concerned a great conflict" – NRSV).

This chapter is actually just the introduction to the prophecy that will be described in detail in chapters 11 and 12. At the time that Daniel wrote this, the first group of captives had returned from Babylon to Judea (see Ezra 1). No reason is given why Daniel was not included among those who returned.

This message came while Daniel was in the midst of a period of mourning and fasting for three weeks. He ate no pleasant food, nor wine nor meat, nor did he anoint himself at any time during this three-week period. We are not told the purpose for this fast, however the result that we will see was that he received another revelation from God.

10:4-6 – Daniel was beside the river Tigris and saw a man clothed in linen with his waist girded with gold. His body was like beryl, his face like lightning, his eyes like torches of fire, his arms and feet like burnished bronze, and his words sounded like the voice of a multitude.

Verse 1 had said that this occurred in the third year of king Cyrus. Specifically, the revelation came on the twenty-fourth day of the first month. Daniel was then by the side of the great river, the Tigris river.

He looked and saw a man clothed in linen with his waist girded with gold of Uphaz. This would appear, of course, to be very valuable clothing. Linen was often used as clothing for people of nobility, royalty, or religious significance (see Leviticus 16:4,23; Ezekiel 9:2; Revelation 19:8; etc.).

The man's body had the appearance of beryl, and his face the appearance of lightning. In other words, it was very bright (compare 12:6,7). Beryl is a transparent pale green, blue, or yellow mineral, sometimes used as a gem.

His eyes looked like torches of fire, and his arms and feet like burnished bronze. Torches of fire again would be very bright, and burnished bronze gleams especially in the sunlight. When he spoke, the sound was like the voice of a multitude. So it would be very loud.

The description of the appearance of this man is obviously intended to greatly impress us that, not only was he someone very important, but he was a messenger from God. The description is in many ways quite similar to that of Jesus Christ in Revelation 1:13-15, so some think this was an appearance of Jesus. See also Ezekiel 1:26-28. The face of Jesus also shown brightly when he was transfigured in Matthew 17:2. Moses' face shown when he came down from the mountain after he had been in the presence of God. Angels are often spoken of as shining brightly.

10:7,8 – The men with Daniel did not see the vision, but they fled with great terror. So Daniel was alone when he saw the vision and no strength remained in him.

When Daniel saw this vision, there were other men with him. However, the other men did not see the vision. Rather, they fled because some great terror fell upon them. We are not told why they fled. Could the meaning be that they saw the man, whose appearance was obviously supernatural and must have been terrifying. So they fled and did not witness the message of the vision.

That left only Daniel to testify regarding what he was told. However, the fact the other men fled shows that they realized some great overwhelming event was occurring. This is similar to the vision in which Jesus appeared to Saul on the road to Damascus: he saw the vision, but those who were with him did not see it – Acts 9:7; 22:9. See also 2 Kings 6:17.

Even though Daniel remained, no strength remained in him. His vigor became frailty, so he acted as though he had no strength but was very frail. Such a reaction to visions, especially visions of such impressive supernatural beings, often had similar effects on those who witnessed them. See Daniel 8:27; Matthew 17:6; Revelation 1:17.

10:9,10 – Daniel heard the sounds of the words spoken, but was in a deep sleep with his face to the ground. A hand suddenly touched him, which made him tremble on his knees and the palms of his hands.

Daniel did hear the sound of the words, but it was as though he was in a deep sleep with his face to the ground. Then a hand suddenly touched him as though to wake him up. But this made him tremble on his knees and the palms of his hands. See also Daniel 8:18; Genesis 15:17.

Again, the description shows how greatly impressed Daniel was with what he saw and heard. And although we were not there, the description also should impress us with how great this being was whom Daniel saw, and therefore how great the end result should lead us to.

No doubt the fact that Daniel had been fasting when the vision occurred would have contributed to his weakness in response to the vision.

10:11,12 – The man said Daniel was greatly beloved and should stand up and understand the message and not be afraid. Since Daniel had humbled himself before God and set his heart to understand, the man came because Daniel's words had been heard.

The man that Daniel saw spoke to Daniel and said that he was greatly beloved. This shows the great respect that God held for Daniel. Note the value of words that assure others that they are loved. God Himself sets the example for us by assuring others of His love.

The comment implies that he was held in esteem in the eyes of God like such men as Abraham and Moses. He should stand upright because the man had been sent to him. Even as he spoke, Daniel stood trembling, but the man said not to fear.

The man said from the first day, when Daniel had humbled himself before God and determined his heart to understand, that his prayer was heard and that is why the man came to speak to him. Notice that the revelation was given, not primarily because of Daniel's fasting, but because of his past history of faithfulness. (Compare 9:22,23; Luke 1:30; 2:10; Revelation 1:17.)

> **10:13,14** – *The prince of Persia withstood the man twenty-one days, but Michael, one of the chief princes, came to help. So now the man had come to help Daniel understand what would happen in the latter days, for the vision referred to many days in the future.*

The man had said that Daniel's words were heard from the time that he humbled himself and set his heart to understand (verse 12). But the man (angel) who was speaking to Daniel had been left alone with the kings of Persia, and the prince of the kingdom of Persia had withstood him twenty-one days. So Michael, one of the chief princes, came to help him.

We are not told exactly who this prince of the kingdom of Persia is. Notice that verse 20 mentions again the prince of Persia and also the prince of Greece. Compare this to earlier verses that use the word "king" to refer kingdoms. Perhaps the prince refers to civil rulers or else symbolizes the nation as a whole as led by their leaders.

It is also not explained how the prince of the kingdom of Persia withstood the man (angel) who spoke to Daniel. Perhaps this means that there was something God wanted this prince to do, but it took a while to persuade him to do it. Finally, he had been persuaded to do what God wanted him to do. What this was I do not know.

Alternatively, some hold the view that the princes of Persia and Greece are spirit beings (presumably demons in service of Satan) who worked to motivate the nations to do evil. This is argued because Michael is here called a prince, and the prince of Persia appears to be distinguished from the kings of Persia, but the commentators especially deny that human rulers could resist an angel.

Aside from the references here to the princes of Persia and Greece (10:13,20), the word "prince" is used as follows in Daniel 8-12: Deity (8:11,25; 9:25), human rulers (9:6,8,26; 11:5,8,22), and Michael an angel (10:13,21; 12:1 – note that 12:1 refers to Michael as the great prince who stands watch over the sons of your people). So the references to the prince of Persia could refer to a human ruler; or if it refers to an evil spirit, it is a different usage from any of these others.

No doubt there are evil spirits working for Satan behind the scenes invisible to us, just as angels work for our good (Ephesians 6:12; 1 Peter 5:8). But I don't know that is the meaning here. There is no reason to doubt that men can resist the power of God; people do it all the time. This occurs because God allows it, not because we have power greater than that of God or angels. The same is true of Satan (Job 1,2). God could wipe out any human or satanic beings at any time, but He chooses not to do so (2 Peter 3:9).

Some claim this refers to war in heaven between angels and satanic spirits. But if this is a war of spirits, why would it be in heaven? The conflict here is on earth. The same is true of Ephesians 6:12; etc.

Why would we assume war happens repeatedly in heaven when the Scriptures describe heaven as a place of peace and joy without evil?

Verses 13,14 do not mean that God was unable to act or to give a revelation to Daniel sooner. God is all-powerful and can do whatever He chooses whenever He chooses. The point is simply that God was waiting for the actions of men before He proceeded. His will and His conduct regarding events on earth often responds to the actions of men.

In any case, Michael, one of the chief princes (an archangel), came to help the man (Daniel 10:21; 12:1; Jude 9). So now the man (angel) had come to make Daniel understand what would happen to his people in the latter days, for the vision referred to many days yet to come.

The reference to the latter days, when spoken by the prophets, would speak to some future time, usually the time of the Messiah. This time was still in the great distant future. It was so used in Isaiah 2:2-4; Micah 4:1-4; Joel 2:28. This latter passage is explained by Peter to be fulfilled in the New Testament or the gospel age. Similar uses are found in other places: see Acts 2:16-18; Hebrews 1:1,2; 9:26; 1 Peter 1:20; 1 John 2:18. See our notes on Daniel 2:28.

But in this case, most of the events predicted here lead up to the gospel age. Remember that these verses are simply introductory to the vision that will be described in chapters 11 and 12.

10:15-17 – Daniel then became speechless till one like a son of men touched his lips. Daniel then said the vision had overwhelmed so he had no strength to speak.

When the man (angel) had spoken these words to Daniel, the effect was so overwhelming that Daniel could not speak but turned his face to the ground. Suddenly someone who looked like a human being touched his lips, enabling him to speak again.

Then Daniel said to the one who had spoken to him that the vision had caused such sorrow to him that he had no strength. He asked how he could talk to the angel, whom he addressed as his lord, when he had no strength nor breath left in him.

It is interesting to observe how even the most faithful servants of God reacted when they received visions from God or appearances of angels when they believed God was speaking to them. Almost invariably they were overwhelmed and usually quite fearful. This is why angels and Jesus Himself, when they spoke to people in such cases, almost invariably began by encouraging the one to whom they spoke to not be afraid.

10:18,19 – The one who looked like a man touched Daniel again. He said Daniel was greatly beloved and should not be afraid, so Daniel was strengthened to speak. He then told the angel to speak because he was now strengthened.

The response to Daniel's request was that the one who looked like a man (presumably the same one as in verse 16) once again touched him and strengthened him. He said Daniel was greatly beloved and should not be afraid. He instructed Daniel to be strong and urged him to have peace or calm.

Exactly how these words had power is not explained, but in any case the result was that Daniel was strengthened. He then said he was strong enough to listen, so he requested the Lord to speak to him.

10:20,21 – The angel then said that he must return to fight with the prince of Persia, and then the prince of Greece would come. He then spoke what is noted in the Scripture of truth and no one upheld him against these except Michael.

So the angel then asked if Daniel knew why he had come to him. He said he must return to fight with the prince of Persia (see verse 13). After he had gone, the prince of Greece would come. He affirmed that what he was saying was recorded in Scripture, and no one upheld these against him except the Prince Michael. This too appears to refer back to verse 13, but is unclear.

It should be clear, as has been stated several times in the book of Daniel, that God is involved in the kingdoms of men. God knows what is happening and He works for His plan to be accomplished.

Note that the angel referred to Scripture as the Scripture of Truth. All Scripture given by inspiration of God speaks truth. We must trust and believe it without doubt.

The use of parentheses in this verse implies that the verse continues into 11:1.

Daniel 11

Vision in the Third Year of Cyrus (continued)

**Wars of Kings Including a Vile Man
Who Defiles the Sanctuary**

A mighty king would oppose Persia but his kingdom would be divided.
Wars continue for many years between kings of north and south.
A vile man will come to power in the north who will plot against the king of the south.
When his plot is foiled, he will rage against the holy covenant.
He will defile the sanctuary, take away the daily sacrifices, and place there the abomination of desolation.
The king shall not regard any god and will blaspheme the true God.
He will enter the glorious land and overthrow many countries, yet he will come to his end.
Many who sleep in the dust will awaken to everlasting life for everlasting contempt.
From the time the daily sacrifices taken away will be 1290 days.
Daniel was instructed to seal up the words till the time of the end.

11:1,2 – The angel then said that in the first year of Darius the Mede he stood up to confirm and strengthen him. He then said that three more kings would arise in Persia, and the fourth would be richer than them all. He would use his strength and riches to stir up all against the realm of Greece.

The fulfillment of the prophecy here and throughout this chapter must be approached differently from the fulfillment of the prophecies in the previous chapters.

The fulfillment of the previous prophecies is recorded in Scripture, giving us inspired commentary to explain the meaning of the prophecy. However, the fulfillment of the events in this chapter occurred during the period of silence between the last Old Testament writer and the beginning of the New Testament record. This leaves us with no information in Scripture to explain the fulfillment.

This means that our only information regarding the fulfillment of the prophecies must come from uninspired history. This may include some secular sources and also apocryphal books, which are not inspired but yet may give some accurate historical insights. I will depend on various sources who have researched this information, including those listed among the sources at the end of our commentary.

Though we must turn to sources outside the Bible to find the fulfillment of the prophecies, we are fortunate to have sources that have recorded the history of this time period. We will find that many of the prophecies in this chapter were fulfilled so amazingly that skeptics who seek to discredit it can only claim that it was written after the events that are described. If in fact the book was written before these events, the detail in the prophecies becomes a powerful evidence for the inspiration of Scripture.

Nevertheless, since we are depending on uninspired history, it follows that we at times may not be certain that we understand all the details correctly. If we had a fuller understanding of history, we might reach different conclusions regarding some details. We must remain open to the possibility of different views regarding specifics, though we can be confident of the general intent of the prophecy.

Note the following quote from Keil, which claims that Daniel's prophecy is not intended to be a detailed description of history. They recognize that a number of details do fit history, but they claim much of it is simply a general outline of the conflict between the Ptolemies and the Seleucids.

> From this comparison this much follows, that the prophecy does not furnish a prediction of the historical wars of the Seleucidae and the Ptolemies, but an ideal description of the war of the kings of the north and the south in its general outlines, whereby, it is true, diverse special elements of the prophetical announcement have historically been fulfilled, but the historical reality does not correspond with the contents of the prophecy in anything like an exhaustive manner.

Subsequent kings of Persia

The NKJV punctuates 11:1 as a continuation of the parenthetical statement in 10:21. The angel who spoke to Daniel at the end of chapter 10 is still speaking to him in the beginning of chapter 11.

The angel states that he had stood up to confirm and strengthen Darius the Mede in the first year of his rule. Darius the Mede was also mentioned in 5:31 and 9:1 (see notes on those verses). He was apparently the Persian ruler appointed over Babylon. The angel said that in some sense he had strengthened Darius.

The angel then predicted that there would be three more kings in Persia, the fourth one being richer than them all. This fourth one would use his strength and riches to stir others up against the realm of Greece.

It is interesting from the outset that the angel was prophesying about the nation of Greece, which was not known as a world empire in Daniel's day. Yet the prophecy predicted the coming of its power.

According to our sources, although Darius the Mede was ruler over the territory of Babylon, the ruler of the whole Persian Empire was Cyrus. The three Persian rulers who would yet arise were Cambyses II (530-522 BC), Smerdis (also called Gaumata or Bardiya, 522 BC), and Darius III the Great Codomannus (522-486 BC). The fourth who would be greater than them all would be Xerxes, who was also known as Ahasuerus in the book of Esther. Apparently Persia did have other minor rulers, but these were insignificant as regards the prophecy, so are not counted. (See also *Archaeology Study Bible*, pages 1225,1226.)

There can be no doubt that Xerxes did lead the Persians to fight against Greece but was seriously defeated at Thermopylae and in the naval battle at Salamis. This is recorded in secular history.

11:3,4 – A mighty king would arise ruling with great dominion according to his will. But his kingdom would be divided into the four directions. It would not be given to his offspring, but the kingdom would be uprooted and given to others.

Following the war between Persia and Greece, a mighty king would arise ruling with great dominion according to his will. This ruler was Alexander the Great who led the Greeks in conquering the Persians and began his own mighty dominion. Alexander was born in 356 BC. He conquered Persia, winning a decisive victory at Gaugamela in 331 BC. He then established the Macedonian Empire.

However, his kingdom would be broken up, separated into the four directions. But it would not be given to his own offspring: that is, he would not establish a continuing dynasty. Instead, the kingdom would be uprooted and given to someone else.

This was fulfilled historically in that Alexander the Great died in 323 BC at the relatively young age of 32. His son was slain, and his kingdom was taken by four different rulers who are not his descendants. These four were: (1) Seleucus (son of Antigonus), who took the Seleucid empire (Syria), (2) Antipater and then Cassander in Macedonia, (3) Lysimachus in Thrace, and (4) Ptolemy I in Egypt.

At first there were various rulers competing for power, but these four eventually dominated. Only Seleucus and Ptolemy will have significance in the rest of the prophecy, because they had impact on Israel. History records a series of six wars in the second and third centuries BC between Egypt (the king of the south) and Syria (the king of the north).

See 1 Maccabees 1:1-10 also Daniel 8:5-21.

> **11:5,6** – *The king of the South would become strong along with one of his princes. Some years later they would join forces because the daughter of the king of the South would seek an agreement with the king of the North. But neither he nor she would keep their power.*

The king of the South would become strong as would one of his princes. The ESV explains that the prince would become stronger than the king of the South and would gain power and dominion over him and have a great dominion. But eventually they would join forces because the daughter of the king of the South would seek an alliance with the king of the North.

However, this alliance would fail. The daughter of the king of the South would not retain her authority, nor would the authority of the king of the North stand. She would be given up along with those who brought her and with him who begot her and with him who gave her strength.

According to the sources, the king of the South was Ptolemy I Soter (son of Lagos). But another prince, Seleucus I Nicator the king of the North became stronger. Some years later, there was an attempt to join forces between the two nations by means of an agreement sealed by a marriage alliance. Ptolemy II Philadelphus gave his daughter Berenice Syra or Phernopherus in marriage to Seleucus Antiochus II Theos.

However, the plan failed in the end. In order to marry Berenice, Antiochus had to divorce his wife Laodice. Various intrigues followed. The father of Berenice died, and Antiochus in turn divorced Berenice to remarry Laodice. Laodice then plotted to kill Antiochus and Berenice and all those who had been involved in the marriage between Antiochus and Berenice. Hostilities between the nations resumed.

> **11:7,8** – *A branch from her roots would come with an army, enter the fortress of the king of the North, and prevail. He would capture their gods and carry them to Egypt along with their princes and precious articles of silver and gold. He would continue more years than the king of the North.*

However, a branch from the roots of the daughter of the king of the South would arise in his place. He would come with an army to attack the fortress of the king of the North. He would enter the fortress and prevail against him. He would take the gods of the people of the north and carry them to Egypt along with their princes and precious articles of gold and silver.

He would then continue longer than with the king of the North. The ESV translates this that for some years he would refrain from attacking the king of the North.

This was fulfilled in the Third Syrian War. Berenice had a brother, Ptolemy III Euergetes, who then became king in Egypt (246 BC) and renewed hostilities. He invaded the North and fought a campaign against Seleucus II Callinicus (or Pogon), son of Laodice, and prevailed. He put to death Laodice for the murder of his sister Berenice. He returned home carrying with him the gods and other treasures from the North. Then hostilities ceased for a time.

11:9,10 – The king of the North would then come to the kingdom of the king of the South, but would return to his own land. His sons would gather a great multitude of forces. One would come and overwhelm and pass through. Then he would return to his fortress and stir up strife there.

The king of the North then would come to the kingdom of the king of the South, but he would return to his own land. The sons of the kings of the north however would stir up strife (the ESV says they would wage war). They would assemble a great multitude of forces and come and overwhelm and pass through. Then one would return to his fortress and stir up strife. The ESV says that he shall carry the war as far as his fortress.

Seleucus Callinicus, the son of Laodice, then attacked Ptolemy in 240 BC. But he was defeated and returned home. His sons, however, renewed hostilities with a great army. The sons were Seleucus III Soter or Ceraunus and Antiochus III the Great, who reigned 223-187 BC. Antiochus attacked provinces controlled by Egypt which by this time was ruled by Ptolemy IV Philopator. This was at first successful, so he returned to Syria. Then he once again attempted to attack Egypt itself.

11:11,12 – The king of the South would then fight with the king of the North. The king of North would muster a great multitude but would be given into the hands of the enemy. His heart would then be exalted, so he would cast down tens of thousands; but in the end he would not prevail.

The king of the South would respond with rage and would go out and fight with the king of the North. The king of the North would muster a great multitude (compare verse 13), but the multitude would be given into the hand of his enemy. When the multitude has been taken away, his heart will be lifted up and he will cast down tens of thousands. But he will not prevail.

When the king of the North, Antiochus III the Great, attacked Egypt itself, the king of the South, Ptolemy IV Philopator, became extremely angry and met him in battle at Raphia. There Ptolemy won a significant victory over Antiochus the Great. However, Ptolemy became extremely proud as a result of his victory. He did not prevail because he simply ceased hostilities and lived in excess.

11:13,14 – The king of the North after the end of some years would come with a great army and much equipment. In those times many would rise against the king of the South. Violent men of your people would exalt themselves, fulfilling the vision, but they would fall.

The king of the North would then make another attempt. He would muster a greater multitude than the first multitude. And after some years he would come with a great army and much equipment. In those times many would rise against the king of the South. Violent men would exalt themselves even from "your people." Since this expression is addressed to Daniel, it would appear to refer to violent men from among the Jews. This would occur in fulfillment of the vision. However, this rebellion also would fail.

Years later (fourteen years), the king of the North, Antiochus III the Great, returned with an even larger army. At this point Ptolemy IV Philopator had been succeeded by Ptolemy V Epiphanes, who was only four years old. People in various other nations joined in the conflict, including some Jews.

The conflict is described in the records of the Jewish historian Josephus. The forces of Egypt were led by a famous general named Scopas.

11:15,16 – The king of the North would build a siege mound and capture a fortified city. The forces of the South would not withstand him: not even with their choice troops. The one who attacked would do as he chose, no one standing against him. He would even stand in the Glorious Land with destruction.

The king of the North would then come and build a siege mound and capture a fortified city. The forces of the South would not be able to stand against him. Even their most choice troops would not have the strength to resist. Rather, the one who came to attack would do according to his will, and no one would be able to resist him. He would even come into the Glorious Land with destruction.

Surely the Glorious Land refers to Israel or Palestine. The implication is that, through much of this conflict and war being described in the prophecy, the Jews would not be directly involved. However, in this case the war would bring destruction even into their own land.

The forces of Egypt were able to push back the forces of Antiochus the Great. However, at Paneas, below Mount Hermon, the battle turned and Scopas was defeated in 198 BC. Scopas fortified himself in the city of Sidon, where his army was besieged by Antiochus and eventually brought into submission. He was not able to resist.

However, according to Josephus, certain Jews had allied themselves with Antiochus in hopes that this would bring them to dominance when Egypt fell. This turned out to be a mistake because Antiochus then turned himself against even the glorious land: that is, Palestine.

> 11:17,18 – *The king of the North will determine to enter with the strength of his whole kingdom. He shall give the daughter of women to destroy it, but she shall not support him. Then he will turn his face to the coastlands and take many. But a ruler shall bring a reproach upon him, the reproach will be removed and he will turn back on him.*

Attempt to control Egypt

The king of the North will continue his war against the king of the South by determining to bring the strength of his whole kingdom against them. The NKJV says he will bring upright ones with him. But the ESV translates differently. It says he shall bring terms of an agreement and perform them. This would imply that he offers terms of surrender.

He shall give him the daughter of women to destroy it. Or as the ESV says, he shall give him the daughter of women to destroy the kingdom. This sounds like he will use the wiles of a woman to attempt to bring down the kingdom of the king of the South. However, it will not succeed. It will not stand or be to his advantage (ESV).

Antiochus determined to rule Egypt itself. Besides force, he had various plots and schemes (perhaps this is the significance of the "upright ones" – perhaps these appeared to be upright but were scheming).

Part of his plan included attempting an alliance by having his daughter Cleopatra I Syra (not the Cleopatra who was involved with Rome) betrothed to the young Ptolemy V Epiphanes. This plan failed, however, because Cleopatra ended up siding with her husband Epiphanes and against her father Antiochus.

Attempt to capture northern territories

Apparently still referring to the king of the North, he would turn his attention to the coastlands and capture many of them. The coastlands in other passages, such as the book of Isaiah, refer to the surrounding nations. Some of these will fall to this king.

Then a ruler shall attempt to bring to an end the reproach against them. When the reproach has been removed, he will turn back on him. Again, the ESV translates: "a commander shall put an end to his insolence. Indeed, he shall turn his insolence back upon him."

The idea appears to be that, the victories of the king of the North are a reproach upon the coastlands. But there is a ruler or a commander who has the power to stand up against this reproach and remove it. This turns the reproach or the insolence of the king of the North back on him.

Frustrated in his attempts to control Egypt, Antiochus then turned his efforts to the northwest attacking into Greece. There he had some success, until finally he was opposed by the Romans who were coming to power. The Romans defeated Antiochus in a series of battles finally culminating in a defeat at Magnesia in 190 BC. Not only was Antiochus defeated, but the Romans took his son Antiochus IV as hostage to assure his future good behavior.

11:19,20 – Then he shall turn his face toward the fortress of his own land, but he shall stumble and fall and not be found. In his place will arise someone who imposes taxes even on the glorious kingdom. But he will soon be destroyed though not in anger or in battle.

Having been defeated in his efforts to capture the coastlands, the king of the North would return home to the fortress of his own land. But even there, he eventually stumbles and falls. That is, he is removed from power.

The defeat of Antiochus at the hands of the Romans was so complete that he was compelled to return to his own land. There he was slain when he was plundering a temple at Elymais (187 BC).

In his place comes someone different. This one places great taxes on the glorious kingdom. The ESV says "the glory of the kingdom." But this does not last long. In a few days he is destroyed, but not as a result of war or hostility.

Antiochus the Great was replaced by his son Seleucus IV Philopator. In order to obtain the large amount of tribute that Rome demanded, he sent a tax collector named Heliodorus throughout the land, including Judea. This is recorded in 2 Maccabees. Eventually Seleucus fell, not in battle, but by treachery perhaps brought on by Heliodorus.

11:21,22 – This one will in turn be replaced by a vile person who does not have the honor of royalty. Nevertheless, he will come with a pretense of peace but will seize the kingdom by intrigue. He will sweep others away from before him with the force of a flood, including the prince of the covenant.

This ruler then in turn will be replaced by still another who is described as a "vile person." He does not have the honor of royalty: that is, he does not come to power rightfully as one who deserves authority. Nevertheless, he will seize power over the kingdom by intrigue or flattery (ESV). He will come in with the appearance of being peaceable or without threat of war.

Those who oppose him will be swept away and broken as by the power of a flood. This would include the Prince of the covenant, who will also be overwhelmed by the power of this vile person.

This was fulfilled by Antiochus IV Epiphanes ("God Manifest") – described as a "vile person" – who came to power in the North. He was the son of Antiochus the Great and younger brother of Seleucus IV Philopator. The rightful heir to the throne was Demetrius I Soter, but Antiochus gained the throne by flattery and intrigue. He was a cruel and tyrannical leader who ruled from 175-164 BC. Daniel 8:9-12 refers to him as the "little horn."

Having come to power, he used his forces to ruthlessly overwhelm all who opposed him. This included the "Prince of the covenant." It is not clear exactly who this is, but some believe it was the high priest in Jerusalem. Antiochus made a treaty with one high Priest, but broke it and made another man high priest. He overwhelmed the city of Jerusalem and plundered the temple. Others believe that the Prince of the covenant refers to Ptolemy VI Philometor, the ruler of Egypt, with whom Antiochus made a treaty.

11:23,24 – He will make a league but will act deceitfully. He will come with a small group of people, entering peaceably even into the richest places of the province, but will do what no ancestors did. He will disperse plunder, spoil, and riches to achieve his plans against the strongholds, but only temporarily.

This vile person will act deceitfully. He will make a league or alliance, but he will come with a small group of people and enter peaceably into the richest places of the province. There he will do what none of his ancestors have done. He will attempt to use plunder, spoil, and riches to accomplish his purposes against the strongholds. But this will last only for a short time.

Antiochus Epiphanes increased his power by making agreements, assisted by a small number of men. He would then maintain favor with his followers by sharing with them the plunder and spoil he obtained by his intrigues. In this way he increased his dominion, coming to power one city at a time. He would promise to come in peaceably, but then would take power over the city.

Meanwhile, he was making plans to overtake the strongholds of Egypt. This would be an achievement that had not been accomplished by his fathers or forefathers. This continued "for a time" – that is, as long as God allowed it.

11:25,26 – He will stir up power and courage against the king of the south with a great army. But the king of the south would oppose him with a very great and mighty army, but he will not stand because of plans devised against him. Those who eat delicacies will destroy him and his army will fall.

This vile person (verse 21) will stir up his power and courage to oppose the king of the South with a great army. The king of the South will respond by bringing into battle a very great and mighty army, but he will not succeed. He will be defeated because people who eat at his own table will devise plans against him and destroy him. His army will be swept away and many will be slain.

Antiochus Epiphanes then proceeded with his plan to attack and capture Egypt. The king of Egypt at that time was Ptolemy VI Philometor, son of Cleopatra and nephew of Antiochus Epiphanes. The Egyptians brought a great army to the battle, but they were defeated by the treachery of their own people. The result was a victory for Antiochus with many Egyptians slain.

See 1 Maccabees 1:17-20.

11:27,28 – Both of these kings will pursue evil, speaking lies at the same table. But this will not succeed, since the end will still come at the appointed time. When he is returning to his land with great riches, his heart will be moved against the holy covenant. He will do damage and return to his own land.

Here the prophecy predicts that the two kings would be committed to doing evil, speaking lies and using deceit in their plans. They would negotiate deceitfully. Their trickery would not succeed, however, but there would still be an end at the appointed time.

When Antiochus had defeated the army of Egypt, the two kings, Antiochus IV and Ptolemy VI, attempted to reach a truce of peace. But both of them were guilty of treachery and neither could be trusted. The truce they negotiated, however, would not succeed because it was not in God's plan for this to happen at this time. Specifically, the Romans were coming to power at this time, and they interfered with the plans of Antiochus, refusing to allow him to loot Alexandria.

King records that, until this time, the Jews had been relatively little involved in the wars between the Seleucids and the Ptolemies. However, a series of intrigues had occurred in Jerusalem by men who sought the high priesthood (Jason and Menelaus). Antiochus was bribed to interfere. This began his involvement in the affairs of Jerusalem, the high priesthood, and the temple.

When returning to his land from Egypt with great riches, Antiochus Epiphanes would be moved against the holy covenant, so that he would do great damage as he returned to his own land. The damage that he did to the holy covenant involved attacks against Jerusalem and the temple.

History records that Antiochus began persecuting the Jews, took away the holy vessels from the temple, slew many Jews and took many captives. He defiled the temple and then returned to Antioch (see 1 Maccabees 1:20-28; 2 Maccabees 5).

> *11:29,30 – At the appointed time he will go toward the south but this time it will be different from the other times. Ships from Cyprus will oppose him so that he is grieved and returns. In a rage he does damage against the holy covenant showing regard for those who forsake the covenant.*

These verses appear to explain in more detail what is referred to in verse 28. At the appointed time (see verse 27) he will once again attempt a campaign against the south. But this time will be different from the previous times. This time ships from Cyprus would oppose him, cause him grief, and force him to return home. As he returns, in his rage he will do damage against the holy covenant. He will likewise encourage people who oppose the service of God according to the covenant.

Once again Antiochus Epiphanes attempted to attack Egypt. However, this time he was not successful as in the previous battles. Ships from Cyprus – Romans ships – opposed Antiochus. This event is recorded in Roman history. A representative of Rome named Popilius met Antiochus near Alexandria and insisted that he return home. He drew a circle around Antiochus and said he could not leave that circle until he agreed to Rome's demands. (See also *Archaeology Study Bible*, page 1229.)

Antiochus returned home in great rage. He vented his fury on Jerusalem and the Jews. Many Jews were slain, but some cooperated with him and were rewarded.

> *11:31,32 – He will muster forces and defile the sanctuary fortress. They will take away the daily sacrifices and place there the abomination of desolation. He will corrupt with flattery those who wickedly oppose the covenant, but those who know God will be strong and carry out exploits.*

This king will muster forces and defile the sanctuary fortress and take away the daily sacrifices. There they will place the abomination of desolation. He will corrupt by means of flattery those who are wickedly opposed to the covenant. People, even in Israel, who are opposed to the true worship of God, he will encourage in their evil. However, those who know the true God will be strong and oppose these efforts with great exploits (they will "take action" – ESV).

In 169-167 BC Antiochus captured Jerusalem, plundered the temple, set up an idol of Zeus in the temple, and demanded that the Jews worship it. This worship even included ritualistic fornication in the temple. He ended the daily sacrifices (Numbers 28:2-8) and polluted the altar by offering swine flesh upon it. He forbade circumcision, forbade observing the Sabbath, and forbade possessing copies of the law. (See also *Archaeology Study Bible*, page 1220,1226.) Many apostate Jews joined him in these persecutions of the faithful (see 1 Maccabees 1:30-67).

Nevertheless, some Jews would remain strong and would resist Antiochus. This may refer to the Maccabees. (See 1 Maccabees chapter 2).

11:33-35 – People with proper understanding will instruct many, but for many days they will fall by sword and flame, captivity and plundering. When they fall, they will receive a little help, but many will join with them by intrigue. Some of these will fall to refine and purify them and make them white until the appointed time of the end.

In this time of damage to the holy covenant, some of those who know the true God and have true understanding (as in verse 32) will instruct many. This appears to mean that they stand for the truth and teach it despite the opposition (they will "make many understand" – ESV). As a consequence of their stand, for many days they will be persecuted and fall by sword and flame, captivity and plundering.

Even in their time of suffering, when they fall they will receive a little help to aid them. Many shall join them by intrigue ("with flattery" – ESV). Among these people of understanding, some will fall. The result of their suffering and persecution will refine and purify them, making them white. This appears to mean that they are proven by suffering to be true and faithful to God. This continues until the time of the end that has been appointed (see again verses 27,29).

Some of the Jewish people remained strong even in the face of persecution at the hands of Antiochus. This included a group called the Hasidim (pious ones). Many of these were put to death. It was at this point that the Maccabees revolted in 168 BC led by Mattathias followed by his five sons. Like all times of persecution, this time separated those who were truly dedicated to God from those who were not. The result refined and purified those who sought to do right.

11:36-38 – The king will do his own will, exalting himself above every god and blaspheming the true God. He will prosper till the wrath has been accomplished and what has been determined will be done. He will not regard the God of his fathers nor the desire of women nor any god, but will exalt himself above them all. Instead he will honor a god of fortresses, gold and silver and precious stones, a god his father did not know.

In his rebellion, this king will do whatever he chooses to do. He will exalt himself as though he is greater than any God, so that he is free to do his own will. He will speak blasphemies against the true God. This will continue till the wrath has been accomplished and what has been determined will be done. "He shall prosper till the indignation is accomplished; for what is decreed shall be done" – ESV.

He does not regard the God of his fathers nor any god, but will exalt himself above them all. Furthermore, he does not regard the desire of women. What does this mean? Perhaps the idea is that he is not influenced by women or the desire for women. He does instead whatever he wants. "He shall pay no attention to the gods of his fathers, or to the one beloved by women. He shall not pay attention to any other god, for he shall magnify himself above all" – ESV.

Instead of honoring gods or women, his god will be fortresses, and he will honor a god his fathers did not know with material wealth: gold and silver, precious stones, and pleasant things. His fathers did not do this, yet he will do so. "He shall honor the god of fortresses instead of these. A god whom his fathers did not know he shall honor with gold and silver, with precious stones and costly gifts" – ESV.

The question to be answered here is what king fulfilled this prophecy. Many theories exist as to who the king is. This is apparently one of the more difficult aspects of the prophecy. Some claim that the prophecy is fulfilled at the second coming of Jesus at the end of time. There is little or nothing here to confirm that view. It is generally held by those of the premillennial persuasion, which we have repeatedly shown to be false.

The Roman Empire?

One explanation that I have heard is that this king refers to the Roman Empire, rather than to one specific man (see Hailey and Harkrider). The description does not seem to fit chronologically with events in the life of Antiochus Epiphanes.

The expression "the king" has been used to refer to an empire, rather than to a specific individual ruler, and in fact has been used to refer to the Roman Empire (7:17,23). We must remember that Daniel has repeatedly made prophecies about the Roman Empire because of its significance in God's plan for bringing Christ into the world. Consider:

* The Roman Empire was the final world empire illustrated in Nebuchadnezzar's dream in Daniel chapter 2.
* The Roman Empire was also the fourth beast in the vision of Chapter 7.
* The Roman Empire was also involved in the vision in Daniel 9:24-27.
* The future prophecies given by Daniel ultimately come to focus in the life and death of Jesus during the time of the Roman Empire. It surely fits the pattern and theme of the book for this prophecy likewise to extend into the time of the Roman Empire.
* In fact the messenger who spoke to Daniel in this prophecy said these things would pertain to the latter days, which is a term for the time of the Messiah (10:14).
* The Roman Empire has already been introduced into this context as those who restricted Antiochus – 11:30.
* This also fits 12:1, which continues the prophecy, as the destruction of the temple in Jerusalem in 70 AD.

The Roman Empire fits the specifics that are revealed in the prophecy here. The Roman rulers surely did according to their own will. Hailey has a lengthy quotation demonstrating the wicked corruption specifically of Nero. He did whatever he wanted, murdering anyone whom he thought stood in his way, including his own wives and other important people.

The emperors exalted themselves above other gods, speaking blasphemies against the true God. In fact, the Roman emperors often claimed to be gods and allowed the people to exalt them as gods. They were infuriated when the Christians and the Jews insisted that there was only one true God, so they refused to worship the emperors. And this continued as long as God willed to allow it to continue. (Revelation 13:5-7)

Rather than respecting the will of the true God, they served the God of war. They built fortresses to protect themselves and to establish military presence among those they conquered. They worshiped this god with their gold, silver, and precious things, not as direct sacrifices, but as the means to pursue their wars. This had not been in the mindset of Rome prior to the beginning of the empire.

Antiochus Epiphanes?

Another view is that the prophecy continues to refer to Antiochus Epiphanes (see King).

* This would certainly fit the context before verse 36, which was definitely referring to Antiochus Epiphanes.
* Antiochus did wear titles that exalted him as God. On his coins he took the title "Theos Epiphanes," meaning God manifest. King says he progressively added divine symbols to the coins.

* Antiochus broke tradition with his ancestors by promoting worship of the god Zeus.

11:39,40 – He shall act against the strongest fortresses by the power of a foreign god. He will cause them to rule over many and divide the land for gain. At the time of the end, the kings of the South and the North will oppose him with great powers. He will enter the countries, overwhelm them, and pass through.

With the help of a foreign god, he will attack the strongest of fortresses. He will acknowledge and advance its glory. This sounds like he is promoting the glory of this foreign god. However, note: "Those who acknowledge him he shall load with honor. He shall make them rulers over many and shall divide the land for a price." – ESV.

The king of the South will attack him, and the king of the North will oppose him with chariots, horsemen, and many ships like a whirlwind coming against him. He shall enter countries, overwhelm them, and pass on. This will happen at the time of the end. We are not told what end. (Instead of "and" the king of the North – NKJV, KJV, ASV, NASB, MLV – several translations say "but" the king of the North – ESV, NRSV, HCSB.)

The Roman Empire?

If this refers to the Roman Empire, then it is not clear what foreign god helped them. Nor is it clear what is the time of the end referred to here. Nevertheless, Rome certainly did come to power over the Ptolemies and the Seleucids, overwhelming them and passing through.

Hailey believes that the god referred to here is the true God of the Bible. He says Rome was accomplishing the will of God, though they did not know it. While this may be true, I see no way to prove that this is what Daniel refers to here. Another possibility is that they served the god of war (verse 38), which was a foreign god in the sense that their ancestors had not served it.

The only time of the end of that I can think would be described here would be the end of the independence of the Seleucid and Ptolemy kingdoms. In other words, when Rome attacked this would be the final fall of those nations. They would be defeated to the point that they became subjects of Rome.

Antiochus Epiphanes?

Antiochus certainly did reward those who supported him by giving them high offices and other rewards. King says that the time of the end refers to the and of the reign of the wicked ruler Antiochus.

The reference to the king of the south and the king of the north would seem to be difficult if the reference is to Antiochus. King attempts to explain it by claiming that the reference is symbolic, as is often the case in describing battles in prophecy. He claims it is simply a summary of battles that have already been earlier described in the prophecy.

11:41,42 – *This king will also enter the Glorious Land and overthrow many countries. But this will not include Edom, Moab, and the prominent people of Ammon. But he will stretch out his hand against countries, and even Egypt will not escape.*

In his aggression, this king will enter and overthrow and occupy many countries. He will even enter the Glorious Land – that is, Israel, the promised land. They too will suffer ("tens of thousands shall fall" – ESV). Other countries he will reach out his hand against, even including Egypt which will not escape.

However, there are some lands that will escape his oppression, including Edom, Moab, and prominent people of Ammon. Why or how these peoples would escape we are not told.

If the fulfillment lies in the Roman Empire, there is no doubt that Rome did invade Judah and defeated Egypt. If Antiochus was the fulfillment, King says the references to Edom and Moab and the children of Ammon are also symbolic since not all those nations existed by this time. Rather, the people who had been part of those nations cooperated with Antiochus in opposition to the Jews. So they did not suffer at the hands of Antiochus.

11:43-45 – *He will have power over treasures of gold and silver and precious things of Egypt. The Libyans and Ethiopians will follow at his heels. But he will hear troubling news from the east and the north, so he will go with great fury to destroy and annihilate many. The tents of his palaces will be planted between the seas and the holy mountain. But he will come to his end and no one will help him.*

In his conquests, this king will take authority over great treasures of gold and silver and over all the precious things of Egypt. Libyans and Ethiopians will follow at his heels: that is, they will be subject to him.

Surely Rome did take great treasures from those whom they conquered. They took spoils of war and tribute money, and so also did Antiochus. Libya and Ethiopia did become subject to Rome. King claims this also is true of Antiochus, however he offers no specific evidence.

He will hear news from the east and the north that troubles him. As a result he will go out destroying and annihilating many with great fury. Rome was always troubled by barbarian invaders such as the Germans and the Huns. Perhaps this is the reference here, some say including the Parthians to the east. King claims that the final years of the life of Antiochus were also spent in attempting to subdue the Parthians.

He will pitch his palace consisting of tents between the seas and the glorious holy mountain. This sounds like the city of Jerusalem. Rome surely did control Palestine even into the time of Christ. They controlled the whole area from Jerusalem to the Mediterranean Sea.

King claims this is once again a reference to events already discussed in the prophecy in which Antiochus brought his armies into Palestine and sought to enforce his laws of religion in worship on the people of Jerusalem. This means that the prophecy does not necessarily proceed in a chronological order.

Nevertheless, for all of his victories, he will ultimately come to his end. When the time comes, no one will help him. He will suffer defeat. And of course, Rome did ultimately fall, though not soon after the events in these verses. God still ruled in the affairs of men. The defeat of Rome is described further in the book of Revelation. And if the reference is to Antiochus Epiphanes, he too came to an end. His forces were repeatedly defeated by the Maccabees, and ultimately he died about that time.

Daniel 12

Vision in the Third Year of Cyrus (continued)

12:1 – Then Michael will stand up, the great prince who watches the sons of the people, and there will be a time of trouble such as never before in the history of the nation. But those who are found written in the book will be delivered.

Michael and those written in the book.

At that time Michael shall stand up. Michael was mentioned in 10:13 (see notes there), and here he is said to be the great prince who stands watch over the sons of the people. Michael is clearly an angel, and the description implies that he was responsible to guard the wellbeing of the people.

There would come a time of trouble such as the nation had never faced before in its history. Then those who were found written in the book will be delivered from the problems. It may sound like Michael was standing up to defend the Jewish nation, but the subsequent verses imply that it was God's people that he defended – i.e., those who are faithful to God, not just those who are physically descended from Jacob.

The Book of Life is the record of those who are saved, destined for eternal life. See Exodus 32:32,33; Psalms 69:28; Daniel 12:1; Malachi 3:16-4:2; Luke 10:20; Philippians 4:3; Hebrews 12:23; Revelation 3:5; 13:8; 17:8; 20:12,15; 21:27. The reference to those who are written in the book shows that the people who are defended are not a physical nation. Rather, it refers to those who are faithful to God.

At that time

"At that time" describes a continuation of the predictions from chapter 11. We have discussed the two possible views that this refers either to the Roman empire or to the desolation caused by Antiochus Epiphanes (11:36-45). "That time" is the time of the end as discussed in the previous section of the prophecy.

The description of a time of trouble refers to trouble such as never had happened in the history of a nation until that time. This is very much like the description Jesus gave when he predicted the fall of

Jerusalem in Matthew 24:15-22; Mark 13:19,20. In His prophecy Jesus referred to Daniel's prophecy in Matthew 24:15; Luke 21:20-22. In that case, the nation here would refer to the Jewish nation.

If this is the meaning, then the delivery of the people who were written in the book would refer to the fact that Christians were watching for the signs of the fall of Jerusalem that Jesus had predicted. He had warned them to flee the city so they would not be destroyed. History records that many did flee and so their lives were spared. They were delivered from the great trouble that the city suffered.

12:2,3 – And many who sleep in the dust of the earth will awake, some to everlasting life, but some to shame and everlasting contempt. Those who are wise will shine like the brightness of the firmament, and those who turn many to righteousness will be like the stars forever and ever.

These verses describe resurrection and rewards. Those who sleep in the dust will awake – that is, they will arise from the dead. Some will receive everlasting life, but some will receive shame and everlasting contempt. Those who are wise will shine like the brightness of the firmament, and those who turn many to righteousness will be like the stars forever and ever.

These verses may seem to describe the final judgment day and eternal rewards. However, we must remember that prophecy is often symbolic, so a spiritual meaning should be considered. If the context refers to the destruction of Jerusalem, then the resurrection here would refer to spiritual resurrection in which many people spiritually received life again from the spiritual death of sin.

Notice furthermore that the passage refers here only to the resurrection of "many," whereas the final resurrection will be a resurrection of **all** the dead (John 5:28,29). Note that the "many" in verse 10 refers to a significant number who would be purified, but it would surely not be all people.

Foy Wallace, in *God's Prophetic Word*, applies this to the persecutions of Antiochus Epiphanes as follows:

> "The reference in these verses is to the vindication of the Jewish cause by the guardian of Israel, designated by Daniel as Michael, who interposed to deliver Israel from the time of trouble. Such a time in the history of Israel is mentioned in Macc. 1:10 and 1:20, 22, 39, and in the history of Josephus. This period was described as the worst time of trouble since Israel was a nation to that time. The description is that of the persecutions of Antiochus Epiphanes, after old testament prophecy was closed and during the period between the testaments. The deliverance that was promised to "every one that shall be written in the book" refers to the fortunes of the Jews who outlived the Antiochus

period of persecution, which is doubtless the sense in which the resurrection is used in verse 2. Some should "awake" from this period of persecution to the everlasting life offered in the gospel, and others to the shame and contempt that accompanied the defeat of the evil cause of Antiochus. The resurrection here compares figuratively with the resurrections mentioned by Isaiah (26:13-19) and Ezekiel (37:1-14) in reference to deliverance from the Babylonian persecution and captivity."

Conversion under the gospel is often described as a spiritual resurrection. Those who remain unconverted in sin are described as being dead in sin because they are separated spiritually from God. When their sins are forgiven by the blood of Jesus Christ, they are reunited with God, which is spiritual newness of life or resurrection. See John 5:25; Ezekiel 37:14; Romans 6:3-8; Ephesians 2:1-6; 5:14; Colossians 2:12,13; 3:1; Luke 15:24,32; Matthew 8:22; 1 Timothy 5:6. Consider also the passages that refer to conversion as a new birth or being born again.

However, just because one is forgiven of sins and spiritually becomes alive again, that is no guarantee that he will remain faithful. The Bible does not teach "once saved, always saved." Some of those who are spiritually raised will persevere to receive everlasting life. But others will fall away in time of temptation and will receive instead everlasting shame and contempt. Jesus specifically predicted that this would happen in the time of the fall of Jerusalem – Matthew 24:10-13.

Those who do remain faithful will shine like the brightness of stars, and their influence will result in turning others to righteousness. The idea of the people of God under the New Testament being like lights in the world is also a common New Testament illustration. This contrasts to those who are in the darkness of sin. See Matthew 5:14-16; Philippians 2:15,16; Ephesians 5:8.

12:4 – Daniel was instructed to shut up the words and seal the book to the time of the end. Many would run to and fro, and knowledge would increase.

Daniel was instructed to shut up the words and seal the book till the time of the end. He was told that many would run to and fro and knowledge would increase.

Shut up the words and seal the book

Shutting up or sealing the book was also mentioned in 8:26 and 9:24 (see notes there). To shut up the book would mean to bring it to a close. This would imply that the message was about to be completed. Daniel had received all that God intended to reveal at this time, so the message should be ended.

A seal in those days was made of a substance like wax placed over the message to keep it closed. This had two purposes: (1) A seal was a sign of ownership, authority, and authentication. It authenticated something as belonging to its owner, usually some important person or official. Seals on a message also authenticated the message as being officially authorized by the sender. The seal would be imprinted with some official symbol indicating its source and authority.

(2) By showing ownership and authority a seal also served to protect what belonged to the owner. It would keep the contents private, protecting it for the one who was intended to receive and read it. If anyone else broke the seal, it would be obvious that unauthorized parties had tampered with the message. For other passages about seals (and rings used for the purpose of seals) see Isaiah 29:11; Daniel 9:24; Revelation 7:2ff; 9:4; Genesis 41:42; Esther 3:10; 8:2; Ephesians 1:13; 4:30; John 6:27; 2 Timothy 2:19; and also Isaiah 29:11; Revelation 10:4; 22:10.

In Revelation 5:1,2, a message on a scroll had been sealed with seven seals and could only be opened by one who is authorized to open the seals so the message could be revealed. Here in Daniel 12, the message was sealed till the time of the end. This would indicate that the message has revealed to Daniel was about to be completed and would be given God's official approval.

However, does this also mean that the message, like the messages in Revelation and in Isaiah 29:11, could not be understood until a certain time? It seems to me that this relates to the New Testament concept of a mystery. Paul often refers to the gospel as a mystery (Ephesians 3:3-5), not in the sense that it could never be understood, but in the sense that the meaning was not clearly revealed until the time of the complete revelation of the New Testament. So a prophecy, like the one Daniel received here, may be sealed, not in the sense that no one else could read it, but in the sense that it would not be understood until a time of greater revelation later. See also 1 Peter 1:9-12.

"Seal (sâtham) – "1) to stop up, shut up, keep close 1a) (Qal) 1a1) to stop up 1a2) to shut up, keep close 1a3) secret (participle) 1b) (Niphal) to be stopped up 1c) (Piel) to stop up" – Brown-Driver-Briggs.

The time of the end

The important question remains as to what time of the end is being referred to. The time of the end was also mentioned in 11:27,35,40; 12:6,8,9,13.

Many assume that this refers to the time right before the end of the world and the final judgment. They try to claim that knowledge is increasing rapidly in our day, so we are close to the time of the end, which they assume means the end of the world.

However, this is simply assumption without proof. We have seen nothing in the context that in any way conclusively indicates that Daniel's prophecy refers to the end of the world and Jesus' second coming. Those who claim this refers to Jesus' second coming invariably proceed to present wild speculations attempting to interpret events that will occur then.

Many attempt even to predict specifically the time when Jesus will return. This, however, is not possible since the Bible clearly says that Jesus will come unexpectedly like a thief in the night. See 2 Peter 3:10; 1 Thessalonians 5:2,4; Matthew 24:34,35; Luke 21:34,35; 12:39,40; Revelation 3:3; 16:15; Mark 13:35.

We have discussed the view that the time of the end refers to the fall of the nation of Israel at the destruction of Jerusalem in 70 A.D. This was the end of the Jewish nation, the end of their form of worship, and the end of their entire system which had existed since the time of Joshua, interrupted by the Babylonian captivity.

If this is the correct view, it would follow that the time of the end here refers to the time of the end of the Jewish nation and the Jewish system. It fell because of their rejection of Jesus Christ. There may be some reason to believe that this also referred to the time of the destruction of the Roman Empire, if that empire is also described in the context, and its fall is predicted in the book of Revelation.

Others, however, hold the view that the context here continues to prophesy about the persecutions by Antiochus Epiphanes. If that is correct, then the end here simply refers to the fulfillment of completion of the time prophesied. It would finally come to fulfillment or an end.

What then is the significance of many running to and fro and knowledge increasing? Speculation has abounded. But let us not accept speculations for which we have no Scriptural evidence and which do not in any way fit the context.

Hailey, King, and others suggest that the meaning could be that many people would look here and there to increase their knowledge so as to understand Daniel's message. The increase in knowledge could occur because events that fulfilled the prophecy occurred in such a way that those who study diligently could understand and gain the knowledge of the meaning of the prophecies.

Surely much of what we have studied here could not have been well understood prior to the various historic events that fulfilled the prophecies. So as knowledge of the events increased, understanding would increase also of the meaning of the prophecy. See Philippians 1:9; Colossians 1:9; 2 Peter 3:18.

12:5-7 – Daniel then saw two others, one on each side of the riverbank. One asked how long till these things were fulfilled. The man in linen swore by Him who lives forever that these things would be finished in a time, times, and half a time, when the power of the holy people has been completely shattered.

As Daniel observed, he saw two others, one on each riverbank. One of them addressed the man who was clothed in linen who was above the waters of the river and asked how long the fulfillment of these wonders would be. The man clothed in linen had been introduced in Daniel 10:5,6. See our notes there.

The man clothed in linen raised both his hands toward heaven and swore by the God who lives forever that it would be for a time, times, and half a time. All these things would be finished when the power of the holy people have been completely shattered.

Of course, this is prophetic language and is highly symbolic. So we must be very careful in our attempts to interpret it. If times, time, and half a time refers to years, then we have 3½ years. If each year is three hundred sixty days (rounded), we have one thousand two hundred sixty days or forty-two months. Verse 11 refers to one thousand two hundred ninety days.

As discussed on 7:25, since these prophecies are highly symbolic, there is little reason to think the time period is literally 3½ years. Some suggest that, since the number seven represents perfection or completeness in Scripture, then half that number (times, time, and half a time equals 3½) may represent a short time which is broken, incomplete, or indefinite.

We also have references to 1260 days (with each month equaling 30 days) described in Daniel 7:25; 8:14. Similar passages are found in Revelation 11:2,3; 12:6,14 13:5. These passages may be helpful. In the book of Revelation, this refers to a period of persecution of God's people but eventually ended in the destruction of the Roman Empire.

This time would continue until the holy people were broken or shattered, then all these things will be completed. Further explanation will be given in the following verses.

12:8,9 – Daniel heard but did not understand. He asked what would be the end of these things, and was told to go his way because the words are closed up and sealed till the time of the end.

Daniel had the same problem that many of us would have. He did not understand the significance of the message. So he asked what would be the end of these things. The response was that he should go away because the words are closed up and sealed to the time of the end. This appears to mean that no further information would be given at this time.

We discussed in Daniel 8:26 and 12:4 the idea of a vision being sealed up or closed up because it refers to the distant future. It is a mystery that will not be understood until later when further information is given. See our notes there for discussion and other similar passages. In this case, the message would be sealed till the time of the end.

The time of the end was also mentioned in 12:4, note verse 13 and see also 11:27,29,35.

12:10,11 – Many would be purified, made white, and refined, but the wicked will act wickedly. None of the wicked will understand, but the wise will understand. From the time the daily sacrifice is taken away and the abomination of desolation is set up there shall be one thousand two hundred ninety days.

The idea of many being purified, made white, and refined was also discussed in 11:35. We concluded there that it meant some would be proven by suffering to be true and faithful to God. Those who suffer persecution and endure faithfully are made better people as a result. So this prophecy would mean that many righteous people would suffer but wicked people would continue to do wickedly.

Those who are wicked would not understand the message, but the wise would understand. God's prophecies are written in a way that hinders the understanding of those who do not have hearts open to the truth. See Matthew 13:13-15. But the wise would understand. The question is: When would they understand? Daniel did not understand at the time the prophecy was given, yet he was clearly wise.

And furthermore, the specific information is given that there would be one thousand two hundred ninety days from the time the daily sacrifices taken away and the abomination of desolation is set up. The removal of the daily sacrifices was mentioned in 8:11,12 and 11:31. Daniel 11:31 also mentioned the abomination of desolation.

In our notes on 11:31, we concluded that this symbolism was used to describe 169-167 BC when Antiochus Epiphanes captured Jerusalem, plundered the temple, set up an idol of Zeus in the temple, and demanded that the Jews worship it. He ended the daily sacrifices and polluted the altar by offering swine flesh upon it. If that is correct, then there would be one thousand two hundred ninety days following this event till the time of the end. That is, this would be a relatively short, indefinite time of suffering and persecution.

If the time of the end, as some view, refers to the destruction of Jerusalem and the end of the Jewish nation or system when Rome destroyed the temple in 70 A.D., this would agree with Daniel 7:25 which uses 3 ½ years to refer to the persecution at the time of the fall of Jerusalem at the hands of the Romans. This would shatter the power of the holy people and bring about the end of all these things (verse 7).

The holy people would refer to the Jewish nation. They were holy, not in the sense of righteous, but in the sense of having been set aside for God's purpose.

God used the Jews as a nation in order to bring Christ into the world to offer the sacrifice whereby people of all nations could be saved. After Jesus came, the nation of Israel no longer had any special purpose in God's plan. And when they completely rejected Christ and crucified Him, this led to their complete downfall as a nation which was accomplished at the destruction of the temple and Jerusalem.

If this explanation is correct, then the twelve hundred ninety days would symbolically represent the time of suffering that accompanied the complete destruction of the temple by the Romans. Daniel refers to the persecution of Antiochus as an abomination that desolates, and Jesus referred to the destruction of Jerusalem by the Romans as an abomination of desolation (Matthew 24:15; Mark 13:14; Luke 21:20). The emphasis is not on the literal or technical meaning of the time length but on the significance of the events.

(Unfortunately, this explanation still leaves some unanswered questions. Verse 7 said it would be times, time, and half a time till the end of all these things. Normally in prophecy that expression would refer to twelve hundred sixty days. So why does verse 11 refer to twelve hundred ninety days? Hailey's conclusion appears to be that the number of days is simply a highly symbolic expression for a time of great persecution and trouble for the people of God.)

12:12,13 – The speaker then pronounced a blessing on the one who would wait and come to one thousand three hundred thirty-five days. But Daniel was to go his way to the end. He would rest and arise to his inheritance at the end of the days.

The message had been sealed. One thousand two hundred ninety days would pass from the end of the daily sacrifice and establishment of the abomination of desolation until the time of the end. But those who are patient and wait an additional forty-five days would be blessed.

Surely thirteen hundred thirty-five days is intended to imply some time that extended beyond the twelve hundred ninety days. If the twelve hundred ninety days ended with the destruction of the temple and Jerusalem in 70 A.D., then some other great event would occur forty-five days later. Again, the time is symbolic, but what is the event to which it refers?

This is difficult. However, commentators whom I otherwise find trustworthy conclude that the longer time period simply refers to those who survive the twelve hundred ninety days of suffering. Depending on one's view, this could be the suffering of the time of Antiochus Epiphanes or the suffering at the hands of the Romans. If it refers to the Roman Empire, this would also fit the prophecies of the book of Revelation. It would also fit the fact that Daniel's prophecies generally look to the time of the Roman Empire and the establishment of Jesus' kingdom.

Rome would bring persecution on the new kingdom that was established by Christ. The establishment of the Messiah's kingdom in the time of the Roman Empire had been described in Nebuchadnezzar's dream in chapter 2 as well as in the vision of Chapter 7. In particular, chapter 7 had described the time of persecution of Christ's kingdom by Rome, which would end with the fall of the Roman Empire.

So Daniel was instructed to go his way till the end. He would rest and arise to his inheritance at the end of the days. This also would be symbolic language. It may sound like a reference to Daniel's receiving his eternal reward. However, another possibility is simply that, when all these prophecies were fulfilled, Daniel would come into his inheritance in that he would be recognized as a true prophet.

The message had come to an end and the book had been sealed. The full meaning would not be understood until the events took place. Until then, Daniel's prophecy would remain in God's inspired record, but it would not come to fulfillment until the time had passed. Then when the time came for the prophesied events to occur, Daniel would receive his inheritance in the sense that his accuracy as a prophet would be established.

Observations on the life of Daniel

The life of Daniel, as recorded in the book, was surely remarkable. Here was a man who lived from the time of his youth till the time of old age serving as an advisor to the rulers of the greatest empires of the day.

He began as an advisor to Nebuchadnezzar king of Babylon in the early days of the Babylonian empire. Later he served as an advisor to Belshazzar at time of the end of the Babylonian empire. He continued serving into the Medo-Persian Empire which succeeded the Babylonian empire. Yet here again he served as a highly respected advisor and public servant.

Yet through all this, he was a Jew living in a foreign land. He advised the Babylonians and the Persians, yet he was neither a Babylonian nor a Persian. He dealt with kings who generally worshiped idols rather than the true God, yet he always remained faithful himself to the true God. And he gave the rulers reason to respect the true God. He faced great opposition and temptation, yet always remained true and faithful.

Despite all this, I can think of not one single event in which the inspired record states or implies that Daniel sinned. Of course, we know that he must have sinned at times since he was human and the

Bible tells us that all have sinned except for Jesus. The Bible record tells us specifically of sins committed by its great heroes including David, Paul, Peter, Noah, Abraham, and Moses. Yet nowhere do I find a record of a specific sin committed by Daniel.

This should give us courage and strength that we can be faithful to God no matter what difficulties we face and no matter how corrupt government becomes. And we can remain faithful even into our old age. There is no need for us to fall away and become unfaithful in our later years as did many kings of Judah.

Studying the life of Daniel should give us strength and courage to serve and honor God faithfully even as he did.

Addendum: Applications to Voting

One of the more challenging issues faced by people who claim to believe the Bible is the question of how trust in God on the one hand relates to man's actions on the other hand. People have mistaken ideas about how faith relates to conduct as regards many aspects of life including salvation from sin, voting in elections, and other aspects of our lives as Christians.

So the purpose of this study is to consider how faith relates to man's actions in voting and many other areas of life according to the teaching of the Bible. Please consider:

Trust and action work together.

People often think that trusting God means people should not or need not do anything. They just trust God and He does it all. However, note just a few passages that show that we must act as well as trust God.

Psalm 37:3 – Trust in the Lord and do good.

1 Timothy 4:10 – To this end we labor, because we trust in the living God.

Galatians 5:6 – What avails in Christ Jesus is faith working through love.

So God does require people to trust Him, but He also requires us to do what we can to accomplish His purposes. When people profess to trust in God so much that they rely upon Him to do everything, they may appear to be so spiritual-minded; but really they have a serious misunderstanding of Biblical faith.

Notice some specific examples in which people believe that trusting God eliminates the need for man to do anything.

Proper Relationship with God

In becoming Christians

Many people believe that we are saved by faith alone. If we trust in God, there is nothing for us to do in order to be saved. "Jesus did it all when He died on the cross." Some even claim that, if we think we must do anything to be saved, we show a lack of faith in God: we are trusting in ourselves, not in God, for salvation.

Such an emphasis on trusting God may sound virtuous, but consider the following passages:

Mark 16:16 – He who believes and is baptized will be saved.

James 2:24 – A man is justified by works, and not by faith only. So as verse 22 explains, faith works together with man's actions. By works faith is made perfect.

These and many other passages demonstrate that true faith in God requires man to obey God in order to be saved.

(See also Matthew 7:21-27; 22:36-39; John 14:15,21-24; Acts 10:34,35; Romans 2:6-10; 6:17,18; Hebrews 5:9; 10:39; 11:8,30; Galatians 5:6; 2 Thessalonians 1:8,9; James 1:21-25; 2:14-26; Luke 6:46; 1 Peter 1:22,23; 1 John 5:3; 2:3-6.)

In maintaining fellowship with God as His children

Many believe that, when Christians commit sins, there is nothing they need to do to be forgiven by God. God automatically forgives an erring child of God, without his needing to do anything. But again, note what the Scriptures teach.

Acts 8:22 – Repent and pray God if perhaps the thought of your heart may be forgiven you.

1 John 1:9 – If we confess our sins, He is faithful and just to forgive us.

So, faith in God does not eliminate the need for people to act. Rather, faith and obedience work together to obtain forgiveness, whether for an alien sinner or an erring child of God.

(See also Acts 8:22; Matthew 6:12; 1 John 1:8-10; Luke 18:13,14; Proverbs 28:13; Psalm 32:1-5; 38:18; 51:1-14; 1 Kings 8:46,47.)

Physical Necessities

Occasionally we meet people who are afraid to make a choice about some important area of life, such as what job to take or where to live, because they fear they may displease God by making a choice different from what He would have chosen.

Matthew 6:11 – Jesus taught us to pray to God for our daily bread. Does this mean we should avoid looking for a job because, if we choose this job in this city, it might not be the choice God wanted?

1 Timothy 5:8 – A man must provide for his own, especially his own household.

2 Thessalonians 3:10 – If a man will not work, neither let him eat.

So although we ought to trust in God to provide our necessities, we also understand that we are responsible to obtain work as the means for providing those necessities. We are obligated to do what we can, then we trust God to use our effort to provide the blessing that we need.

Most people can understand this, but many struggle in other similar areas.

Care for Health and Life

3 John 2 shows that we should pray for good health.

Some believe trusting God for health means we leave everything to Him.

Some conclude that going to a doctor shows a lack of trust in God. Near Ft. Wayne there was a religious cult in which several children died, because the parents believed they should just trust God for healing, instead of taking their children to a doctor.

I read a book in which a child died in a car accident. The mother comforted herself by believing that, even if the child had not been in the accident, she would have died anyway because God had determined that her time had come to die. Such ideas may sound like supreme trust in the will of God, but consider:

What does the Bible teach?

Colossians 4:14 – The Bible tells us that Luke was a physician.

Luke 5:31 – Jesus Himself said that those who are sick need a physician.

2 Corinthians 12:7-10 – Paul prayed three times for God to remove his thorn in the flesh. Later he learned that God did not will to remove it, but did Paul do wrong in praying the prayer? Would Paul have sinned if he had gone to the physician Luke to help remove the problem before God revealed His will in the matter?

Using the services of people with special health training is not contrary to trust in God. At times God may not choose for us to get better, but we can't know that ahead of time. In fact, the doctor may be the very means God uses to answer our prayer for health!

This illustrates the fact that there are many specific aspects of our lives for which God's specific will simply has not been revealed. So, we must do what we believe to be best, even as we pray for God to bless our efforts. Trusting God does not contradict working to bring about what we pray for, but rather faith works together with our efforts.

Number of Children

Some people believe they should leave the number or spacing of their children completely up to God.

They believe it shows a lack of faith in God to use artificial means to avoid conception.

The fact is that a man and his wife cannot possibly leave such a matter entirely up to God. They necessarily do make choices that affect whether or not they conceive. They are the ones who decide to have the physical relationship or not! It makes no sense to say that they leave it entirely up to God, when they know that their action is necessarily involved.

What does the Bible say?

Genesis 1:26-28 – At creation, after He made male and female and told them to reproduce, God immediately said man was in charge of the earth and everything on it. "All the earth" is under our dominion to use for our good (verse 26). That would include our own bodies (verse 28).

Surely it is wrong to kill a child that has been conceived. But using artificial means to control when and how often a married couple conceive is no different in principle from any other medical treatment. Some use medical means to try to help when they are having trouble conceiving, and others use medical means to avoid conceiving when they are not ready.

So, we should pray to God and trust Him, but we know that He has not specifically revealed how many children we will have or when. So we should do what we can, then we should trust God to use our choices for good according to His will. Such actions do not inherently contradict faith in God any more than any other decision about physical health or blessings.

Choosing Rulers

Daniel 4:32 – The Most High rules in the kingdom of men and gives it to whomever He chooses.

1 Timothy 2:1,2 – We should pray for rulers. So some claim we should pray but not vote, because we might vote for someone different from the ruler God wants. We should just leave such matters entirely up to God.

Such reasoning may sound like trust in God, but they are exactly parallel to all the other views we have discussed.

What does the Bible teach?

Esther 7:1-10 – A godly woman used her influence to bring down a wicked ruler. Was she wrong? Should she just have prayed and done nothing, leaving the matter entirely up to God? The main point of the book is that, instead of doing nothing, she had the courage and wisdom to act for the good of her people, even though she did not know what the outcome would be (4:6-17). [This is an Old Testament example, but so is Daniel 4:32.]

Acts 22:24-29; 23:12-33; 25:10-12; 16:35-40 – The apostle Paul often used his rights as a Roman citizen to work for his own protection and to help further the gospel. Our government gives us the right to voice our views about who should govern us and about the laws they make. If Paul used his rights to protect himself and help further the gospel, why should we not use the right to vote? Can we not thereby help protect ourselves and our families from harm, help maintain our freedom to preach and practice the truth, and even help bring down wicked rulers like Esther did?

We are accountable to obey only what God has revealed in Scripture.

God does not impute sin to men when they act with good intention in matters regarding which God has not revealed His will (Rom. 4:15; 5:13). But in the areas we have discussed, God has not revealed His specific will regarding affairs on earth. We should pray to Him and trust Him, but we should also do what we can to bring about the answer to our prayer, acting in harmony with the general principles God has revealed.

In the end, God may choose some outcome different from what we worked for. We may not get over that sickness (like Paul in 2 Cor. 12), we may not have the child we hoped for, or the ruler we voted for may lose. In such a case, we should accept His will (Matthew 26:36-46). But working to do what we believe to be best is not wrong nor does it show lack of trust in God, since He has not revealed His will in such matters. (Consider Esther 4:13-16.)

In all the areas we have discussed, the idea that faith in God means we must leave everything up to God is a Calvinist concept.

Not everyone who believes these things is a Calvinist, but these ideas are based on Calvinistic-like thinking. Pure Calvinists believe that God has decreed from eternity everything that will happen, so they believe nothing they do can affect anything. God determines it all.

So the ideas we have discussed may sound like great faith in God, but they are all based on unbiblical concepts, even though many who hold these concepts would never consider themselves to be Calvinists.

The proper approach in such matters is to study what God **has** revealed. If His specific will is not revealed in some area, we should make a choice based on our best information, then pray to God to bless our actions to produce the outcome He desires.

Sources Frequently Cited in These Notes

Ancient Christian Commentary on Scripture; InterVarsity Academic, Downers Grove, IL, 2006. WORDsearch CROSS e-book

Archer, Gleason, Jr., *A Survey of Old Testament Introduction*; Moody Press, Chicago, IL, 1964.

Barnes, Albert, *Barnes' Notes on the Old Testament;* WORDsearch CROSS e-book, 2010

ESV Archaeology Study Bible, The; Crossway, Wheaton, IL, 2017

Exell, Joseph S., *Biblical Illustrator, The;* 1900, Public Domain

Free, Joseph P., *Archaeology and Bible History,* (11th edition); Scripture Press Publications, Wheaton, IL, 1972

Hailey, Homer, *A Commentary on Daniel: a Prophetic Message*; Nevada Publications, Las Vegas, Nevada, 2001

Harkrider, Robert, *Daniel: "God Rules in the Kingdom of Men"*; Norris Book Company, Russellville, AL, 1985

Holden, Joseph H. and Norman Geisler, *The Popular Handbook of Archaeology and the Bible*; Harvest House Publishers, Eugene, Oregon, 2013

Horne, Thomas, *Introduction to the Critical Study and Knowledge of the Holy Scriptures*, 4 volumes; T. Cadwell, Strand, London, 1828 (public domain)

Keil, C. F. and Franz Delitzsch, *Commentary on the Old Testament;* originally published by T. and T. Clark, Edinburgh, 1866-1891

King, Daniel H, Sr., *Truth Commentaries: The Book of Daniel*; Guardian of Truth Foundation, Athens, AL, 2012

Millard, Alan, *Nelson's Illustrated Wonders and Discoveries of the Bible;* Thomas Nelson Pub., Nashville, TN, 1997

Pfeiffer, Charles F., *Baker's Bible Atlas*, Baker Book House, Grand Rapids, MI, 1961

Price, Randall with H. Wayne House, *Zondervan Handbook of Biblical Archaeology*; Zondervan, Grand Rapids, MI, 2017.

Waldron, Bob and Sandra, *A Remnant Shall Return: Captivity, Return, Years of Silence;* Bob Waldron, Athens, Alabama, 1996

Wallace, Foy E., Jr., *God's Prophetic Word,* Foy E. Wallace, Jr. Publications, Oklahoma City, OK, 1946

Young, Edward J., *An Introduction to the Old Testament*; Wm. B. Eerdmans Publishing Company, Grand Rapids, MI, 1960.

Printed books, booklets, and tracts available at
www.gospelway.com/sales
Free Bible study articles online at
www.gospelway.com
Free Bible courses online at
www.biblestudylessons.com
Free class books at
www.biblestudylessons.com/classbooks
Free commentaries on Bible books at
www.biblestudylessons.com/commentary
Contact the author at
www.gospelway.com/comments
Free e-mail Bible study newsletter
www.gospelway.com/update_subscribe.htm

Made in the USA
Las Vegas, NV
10 October 2021